Designed Change Process:

Managing Stress, Feelings and Behavior

Bob Schoenberg

Heuristic Books

Chesterfield, Missouri USA

Publisher's cataloging information:
Designed Change Process: Managing Stress, Feelings and Behavior
    Schoenberg, Bob.
  Designed Change Process / Bob Schoenberg.
  Includes bibliographical references.
  ISBN 978-1-59630-080-4 (alk. paper)
    1. Decision making. 2. Problem solving. 3. Organizational
effectiveness. 4. Success in business. 5. Change Management.

Heuristic Books

is an imprint of

𝕾cience & 𝕳umanities 𝕻ress
PO Box 63006
Chesterfield MO 63006-7151
636-394-4950
Heuristicbooks.com

Heuristic Books
for Mathematics & Management Science
heuristicbooks.com

Dedication

This book is dedicated to the memory and teachings
of Tom Sargent

Acknowledgements

There are several people I wish to thank. First, I wish to thank Niek Sickenga for his support and encouragement. I thank Carmen Winslow, City Editor of *The Montana Standard – Butte, Mont.* for allowing me to print Tom Sargent's obituary. I thank Linda Sargent Reinfeld for giving me permission to print a photograph of Tom from her website.

I also wish to thank Peter Sargent, son of Tom Sargent and Cathy Sargent, daughter of Tom Sargent, for allowing me to publish various materials from Change Agents.

Finally, I wish to thank my publisher, Bud Banis, for publishing this book and making it possible for others to read it.

Foreword:

One of the benefits of Bob Schoenberg's book about Tom Sargent and his Designed Change Process is, that besides Tom's invention and development of the Designed Change Process, we are back in the beginning of the time slot of the seventy's of last century. That was another time than we enter now. World War II was over, the Vietnam war was on, and we were digesting the 1960's with all the changes, especially those about authorities and respect. In that time, the years 2000 and later, were still far away.

Now, looking back at Tom's designed change processes of those days, and as they developed, and also the practice of the unlearning of 'automatic behavior', are both still almost actual and useful for the time to come. Nowadays we have to prepare ourselves to live in the era of the two thousand twenties!

So how did they do it in the seventieth of last century? What did they learn and where do we start now! Bob Schoenberg was there and gives now his vision.

I met Tom Sargent only once. That was at the celebration of the 25th anniversary of the CCI approach in 1999 at Hartford (CT) on April 18th. He was one of the three founders of the CCI co-counsel approach, that developed into an unfolding vision of a way of living in peace with your past, present and future. We had no time to share, I had to ran to the door and just was able to shake hands with him. As a wordless compliment, to honor his initiatives and – as I was told – his famous guided meditations.

For all those who want to become aware of whatever, I highly recommend you read – and reread – this book. Check and share your own reactions on what this book hands over to you and discover how it may support your life!

Niek Sickenga
editor (www.) CCI World News Service

Contents

Introduction

Tom Sargent was my mentor, colleague and friend. I had personally trained and studied with him. Over the years, I had lost contact with him, but always thought about him. When I learned of his passing (two years after the fact), I decided I wanted to do something to perpetuate his teaching. This was a man who had helped so many people and had ideas and information that continue to impress people even today.

At first I considered writing a biography about Tom. As I began to research this man's life, it became clear to me that a book about his teachings would be much more beneficial to people and would be a much greater service than a book about him.

I had in my possession many of his writings and the knowledge that I had learned when I trained with him and worked with him – many years ago. I decided to write a book about his teachings, namely the Designed Change Process. Tom was a great teacher and wrote many handouts that were easy to comprehend. However, the one book he wrote was written in somewhat of a scholarly manner and was difficult to comprehend. I decided that I would "translate" his book and make it "user friendly". I also supplemented my writing with several of his handouts and other documents that I had in my possession.

As I began writing this book, I soon found myself reliving many of the training sessions I had with him. I have shared many of these experiences in this book. It is not just an explanation of the Designed Change Process. It is also a personal glimpse into the actual training, my memories and some of my own stories as well.

It all began when I was in my senior year of undergraduate school at the University of Hartford. I was a volunteer at a crisis and intervention center in 1974. We were all peer counselors. None of us were therapists or professionals. When we ran into a problem that was beyond our capability, we referred to our consultant – Tom Sargent.

Eventually, I decided to enroll in one of Tom's Life Enrichment Groups. I ended up doing all three of the groups and eventually enrolled in his training program. It was a competency based training program where you had to really demonstrate competency in the skills and information. There were no quizzes or tests, but, you had to demonstrate actual competency in use of the material and skills. When I finished the final phase, I was offered an opportunity to become the Program Director of the New England Humanistic Education Center. Eventually I became the Director and ran that Center for five years, teaching teachers the same information that Tom taught in his Life Enrichment Groups and his Training Institute, which eventually became known as the Designed Change Institute, and the material became known as the *Designed Change Process.*

The information that Tom had been developing and teaching for several years was eventually put into his book and was called the Designed Change Process, (D.C.P.). This Process focused on three important areas: Self Esteem, Feelings and Behavior. Tom was a master at teaching people about feelings and how to change them. He also created a concept of what he called "ME", which he never really defined. "ME" was synonymous with a strong sense of self esteem and self image. Tom created an entire group/workshop called "Celebrate ME". He had an

2

amazing ability to teach people how to interrupt and change their behavior patterns. These three topics became a central part of the D.C.P. This book is about the Designed Change Process and other teachings that I learned from him.

The Designed Change Process is based upon the "integration of methods developed from Alcoholics Anonymous" (Sargent 1984, 129) and after years of research that was originally developed by Tom Sargent as a result of his experience with Alcoholics Anonymous and Al-Anon Family Groups (Sargent pp.3). According to Sargent (1984), "the AA recovery process was conceptualized and systematized and was first taught to a group of recovering alcoholics (AA members) who were working with alcoholic patients at Montana State Hospital" (3).

After the experience at the Montana State hospital, the D.C.P. was used with other people besides alcoholics. A central concept of the D.C.P. was "stress reduction for clarity as well as for flexibility …" (Sargent, 1984 4). The reduction of stress allowed self determined solutions to problems (4).

In 1974, I was given a copy of Sargent's self published training manual where he identified, "distress distorts". This continued to be a major theme in Mr. Sargent's teaching and training. The Process eventually was found to be useful in a variety of settings, including counseling, education, medicine, medical emergencies, law enforcement and the high tech industry.

An important part of the D.C.P was the Bimodal Model of Behavior, which will be discussed in more detail in a later chapter. Essentially, the Bimodal Model explained human behavior in terms of two different types of behavior – Aware and Programmed. Aware behavior is flexible, present and intentional. Programmed behavior is fixed, past and automatic.

While all this may sound technical and difficult to understand, it was taught in a very simple, easy to understand manner, which will be described later. Sargent, who ran a counseling and consulting center, originally known as "Change Agents", offered a variety of classes, groups and workshops. Participants were taught the following information about distress:

1. Distress Distorts Perception

2. Impairs Thinking

3. Triggers automatic responses (habits) often learned from an earlier time in one's life.

The D.C.P. distinguished between "stress" as external, and "distress" as internal and offers numerous ways to reduce the effects of distress. Selye defined distress as any uncomfortable feeling (Selye, 1974). Another key component of the D.C.P. was self esteem enhancement. Sargent had an entire class which he called "Celebrate ME" that provided participants with self esteem training. The training included a guided imagery with built in associations enabling people to instantly recall and access any part of the guided imagery and use it in a real life situation. This was and continues to be quite different than the use of other guided imageries, which continue to be popular today.

Sargent was a master at teaching people about feelings – what they are and how to "manage" them. This was another key part of the D.C.P. and was commonly referred to as the Feelings class or workshop. Out of this material an entire workshop was created on Stress Management by this author.

In addition, there was also an Inter-Personal Relations class which in the D.C.P was called "Interpersonal Dynamics" (Sargent, 1984 51).

The emphasis of the D.C.P and of the Bimodal Model focused on the problems pertaining to "unlearning". "Learning to unlearn requires improving the familiarity with the self and skill with interrupting undesirable behavior" (Sargent, 1984 85). Participants were taught to use both modes of behavior: Aware and Programmed modes.

Each component of the D.C.P. will be discussed in subsequent chapters. In addition, other applications of this Process will be discussed as well.

Overview of Chapters

In Chapter One, I discuss the Bimodal Model of Behavior. Here you will learn that there are two basic modes of behavior. One is Intentional and the other is Automatic. Both are essential to are existence. However, the Automatic mode often contains outdated or inappropriate behavior patterns which are rigid, repetitive and allow very little choice.

In Chapter Two I discuss Stress vs. Distress. Not only is there a difference, but distress has a profound effect upon the body and the mind. In the 21 century, it seems that everyone is stressed. A little bit of stress can be useful. But, too much stress can actually be harmful and has a definite effect, which is not a good one.

Chapter Three describes the "Celebrate ME" workshop and provides a variety of ways to enhance one's sense of self-esteem. The idea of "celebration" is explained and many techniques are introduced to promote a solid sense of self.

Chapter Four provides fascinating, yet useful and practical information about Feelings. What feelings are, what they do and how you can change them are explained. Much of this information became the basis for a Stress Management Program that I created.

Chapter Five explores the relationship of Inter-Personal Relations. The critical role that stress and behavior patterns play in relationships is explored and specific techniques are offered for improving relationships.

Chapter Six traces the history of Co-Counseling and discusses Tom's integration of the concept of 'Celebration' into Co-Counseling. How Tom adapted various co-counseling technique for training purposes, which proved highly effective, is also discussed.

Chapter Seven explains the concept of Unlearning, which requires several components of the Designed Change Process and a certain level of skill.

Chapter Eight discusses various applications of the Designed Change Process and how they are used.

Overview of Appendices

Appendix A – flyers of actual workshops and classes offered at Change Agents using the Designed Change Process.

Appendix B - provides a brief biographical sketch of Tom Sargent and a description of the Change Agents Training Center, which includes a physical description of the building that housed his work, office and training.

Appendix C – About Bob Schoenberg and the Designed Change Process.

Chapter 1 – The Bimodal Model of Behavior

Tom Sargent ran a counseling/consulting center in Hartford, CT. Prior to and during this time he and some of his staff members developed the Designed Change Process, (D.C.P.) In 1984 he wrote and self published a book, called the <u>Behavioral and Medical Effects of Stress</u> (no longer in publication), which was a scholarly description of the D.C.P. This publication that you are reading is a "user friendly" description of that Process.

A central part of the Designed Change Process, (D.C.P.) is the Bimodal Model of Behavior. This model describes two different types of behavior – "Aware" and "Programmed". We actually use both types and the D.C.P. teaches how to intentionally use both programmed behavior, which is rigid, repetitive and unaware and the aware mode which is flexible and offers a maximum of choice. What follows is a description of this Process.

The Bimodal Model of Behavior

The Bimodal Model of Behavior of the D.C.P. is described by Sargent (1984) as "Aware and Programmed functions (15). The Aware Function is Flexible, Present and Intentional. Included in this function is a high sense of self esteem represented by the word "ME" with lines shooting out like rays of the sun (see figure 1).

The Programmed Function is Fixed, Past and Automatic. Included in this function are the words, "current, culture and childhood".

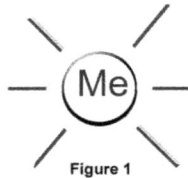

Figure 1

I have since adapted the model as follows. There are two forms of behavior:

Automatic and Intentional.

The Automatic is unaware, rigid and no choice.

The Intentional mode is aware, flexible and maximum amount of choice.

AUTOMATIC	INTENTIONAL
Unaware	Aware
Rigid	Flexible
No Choice	Maximum amount of Choice

The Automatic Mode

Behavior here is automatic and little if any thought goes into it. It is like a computer program. It just runs. There is little if any awareness. The behavior is also rigid. It's the same every time. Finally, this is no choice, because the behavior is automatic. Automatic behavior can be triggered by various types of stimuli, especially distress. The more distressed a person becomes the greater likelihood that an earlier learned behavior will be triggered. Oftentimes an individual will resort to childlike behavior. It is an automatic response.

The Intentional Mode

Under this mode, behavior is intentional. One is aware and flexible and has a maximum amount of choice. If one has awareness one can choose what to do as opposed to being unaware and having a behavior pattern run much like a computer program does. Because one is aware, there is flexibility and a maximum amount of choice. One could even choose to go into automatic behavior! This statement requires an explanation.

Why Automatic Behavior is Useful

Automatic behavior is incredibly effective. Much of human behavior is very complex and automatic once it is learned. Consider all the various actions one must do to drive a car. First, one must open the door of a car. If the car is locked, a key or a remote door opener must be used. Then the person must move out of the way of the door in order to open it. Next, one must get into the car. Think about how you do this. Do you literally step onto the floor of the car and sit down or do you sit down and slide your feet around?

Then one must insert the key into the ignition and turn the key to start the engine. Usually, one must have a seatbelt on in order to do this. Then there is the matter of applying pressure to the brake. When I first learned how to drive, the car would buck like a wild horse. Eventually, I learned how to apply just the right amount of pressure on the brake pedal so the car came to a stop smoothly. Learning to shift gears, even with an automatic transmission is yet another piece of behavior.

We take all these bits of behavior (and there are many others that I didn't list) and we "chunk" them together and call it driving a car. Once we learn how to do this, it all becomes automatic. We no longer think – okay, open the door, get in, put on the seatbelt, insert the key and start the engine. All of this is automatic. This is an example of a useful automatic behavior. Walking, talking, and writing are all examples of automatic behaviors that we have learned.

If we had to consciously think about how to walk or talk or write, we wouldn't be able to function. So many automatic behaviors are not only useful, but also essential.

The problem arises when we engage in an automatic behavior that is no longer appropriate or is outdated. This sometimes happens when we get a new car and the controls are located in different locations. We tend to do what we have done before until we learn the new location of the controls. However, in some situations the old behavior is so ingrained that we respond automatically. This is especially true when we get distressed. Imagine that you had your bed against a wall right next to the light switch on the wall. However, during the summer you moved your bed to the opposite wall where it would be a little cooler. You wake up and need to use the bathroom, but you know you are not near the light switch. So, you grab your flashlight. Then one night you are awoken by a noise that sounds like someone is trying to break into your home. You jump up and reach for the light switch. A few moments later you realize the light switch is on the opposite side of the room. Other times, however, one might intentionally choose to go into automatic behavior because it requires little if any thinking once activated.

Why Intentional Behavior is often essential.

When we want to solve a problem, learn something new, develop a relationship or do anything that requires our attention, we need to use Intentional Behavior by itself or combine it with Automatic behavior. Oftentimes we need to be aware of what is happening and decide how to respond, rather than respond automatically. Intentional behavior actually allows us to change our automatic behavior, which is often referred to as a "behavior pattern" or a habit. As mentioned previously, sometimes we might choose to intentionally use an automatic behavior. But often this requires some training, which is provided as part of the Designed Change Process (D.C.P.)

According to the Bimodal Model, we use both types of behavior. The difficulty arises when we try and change automatic behavior, because much of our automatic behavior is done on an unaware basis. Sargent (1984) identifies changing the "Programmed Function" as "unlearning", which is an important component of the D.C.P.. A simple way of explaining this is that "unlearning" means deliberately changing a habit or automatic response. To do so requires using Intentional behavior and a strong sense of Self which Sargent refers to as your "ME". The concept of a strong sense of self ("ME") will be discussed in a later chapter.

The Use of Filters

Sargent identified in his Model that filters affect which mode of behavior is selected. He provided a rather complex description and explanation of this and I will attempt to simplify it. In one sense, feelings act as filters. If I'm depressed, I see things in a dark and gloomy way. Such a viewpoint can affect not only how I feel, but can also greatly influence how I act. In the original model, Sargent shows an arrow going through a filter. The arrow then splits with part of it going into the Automatic mode and another part going into the Intentional mode. Filters are discussed in greater detail in the chapter on Feelings.

However, for purposes of this discussion, it is important to understand that the various filters we have influence our behavior. While I have described the effects of one filter (depression), the fact is we have numerous feelings that influence out behavior. Regardless of what happens, oftentimes that stimulus is filtered and that creates a unique perception for us. If we perceive that we are being threatened in any way, distress results. Once we perceive distress, the Automatic mode of behavior is activated. If on the other hand, we perceive something that is non-distressing, the Intentional mode of behavior is activated.

It should be noted, that generally, it is not possible to go from Automatic behavior to Intentional behavior without specific training or until the distress feeling subsides. The topic of "filters" delves into discussions about reality vs. perception. Oftentimes, what exists is not necessarily what we see. We do know that when we are distressed our perception is altered. But there are other factors that could influence one's perception.

Recent research by this author indicates that frames of reference, or more commonly known as a point of view or a perception can greatly influence our thinking, (Schoenberg, "Frames of Reference" in Critical Thinking in Business 2007). Such filters could be either feelings or thoughts. Feelings are recalled by thoughts and thoughts usually have some feelings attached to them. Therefore, practically any stimulus will evoke either a thought or a feeling. We tend to make associations or connections between unrelated events or items. For example, there doesn't appear to be any connection between a building and a headache. However, if I had a bad headache I might recall that I happened to be looking at a building at the time and make an association between that building and my headache. Even though there is no connection, in this way of thinking there is a connection. I recall I had a bad headache when I looked at a particular building. Now every time I see that building I recall the headache I had, although there is no cause and effect here. The building did not cause my headache. But, every time I see that building I am reminded of the headache I had.

The information about filters, perceptions and associations gives one a glimpse into the complexities of human behavior. To put all of this into perspective, filters can affect which mode of behavior we use.

In summary, there are two different types of behavior: Intentional and Automatic. Intentional behavior includes awareness, flexibility and a maximum amount of choice. Automatic behavior includes little or no awareness, rigidity and no choice. Both types of behavior are used. Automatic behavior is very efficient because it requires little if any thinking. However, sometimes the automatic response is outdated or inappropriate.

Intentional behavior requires thinking and provides a maximum of choice. In essence, both types of behaviors are essential. However, Intentional behavior is required in order to change Automatic behavior (habits). One of the main features of the D.C.P is the ability to change habits. The changing of a habit is called "unlearning' and requires a strong sense of Self which is referred to in the D.C.P. as "ME".

The D.C.P. initially consisted of three Life Enrichment groups that were later called "workshops". These three workshops: *Celebrate Me, Feelings* and *Inter-personal Relations* form the basis for much of the training of the D.C.P. Each one of these workshops will be discussed in a separate chapter.

In later years, the D.C.P. focused on "pattern interruption" also known as the changing of unwanted habits or "Unlearning", as it came to be called. A separate chapter will discuss this topic in detail.

Practical Applications

Essentially, there are two types of behaviors: Automatic and Aware. We need and use both of these behaviors. The Automatic mode is very efficient and practical. A great deal of our behavior comes from this mode. Practically anything we have learned to do becomes an automatic behavior. Such behaviors as walking, talking, driving a car, dancing, playing a game of chess are all examples of Automatic behavior. Even more complicated things such as giving a presentation, writing a report, doing math calculations, using a computer, and most professions all use automatic behavior. In fact, every job requires you to learn a format, procedure or way of doing something and eventually these learned actions become automatic. If they don't you will probably be terminated by your employer.

However, as discussed previous, some learned behaviors are no longer appropriate or are outdated. For example, Harry learned as a child that if he screamed and yelled, he would often get his way. Today, Harry is an adult who works as an editor of a newspaper. Usually Harry is reasonable and treats his employees with respect. However, when Harry gets distressed, he yells and screams and oftentimes employees do whatever he wants just to get him to stop screaming and yelling at them. (Note: Harry is a fictional character created to illustrate a point as are the other characters mentioned in this book).

Consider Susan, who for years was overweight until she learned how to change her eating habits. Susan normally maintains a weight that satisfies her. However, when she becomes really distressed, she reverts back to her old habits, which not only includes eating as a way to manage stress, but also reverts back to old thinking patterns that she will always be overweight and that nothing works for her. For a while it appears that Susan has lost the information and knowledge she has about successfully losing weight and maintaining that weight.

In each of the above examples, we see that distress can trigger an old pattern of behavior. It's almost as if the current information a person has is temporarily disconnected while the "patterned behavior" (Automatic) runs. As each person calms down, they are then able to think clearly and realize what is happening. That is when the Intentional Behavior occurs.

Intentional Behavior

Using this mode of behavior one has a maximum amount of choice, is aware and flexible. To return to Harry, when he's in the Intentional mode of behavior he realizes that he has several different options. He doesn't need to scream and yell. He is flexible and he is aware of several options and choices. But, when the Automatic behavior runs, he has little awareness, is inflexible and just runs the behavior pattern. It may seem to Harry that there is nothing he can do, but this is not accurate. With training and practice, one can learn to use both modes of behavior. Oftentimes people get the false impression that Automatic behavior is "bad" and is to be avoided. This isn't true. Automatic behavior is essential. If we had to stop and relearn everything we did, to analyze it and figure it out, we wouldn't be able to do much of anything. As I write this text, I am using Automatic behavior. I know how to write and type. I know how to create sentences and paragraphs.

However, I'm also using some Aware Behavior as well. Yes, it is possible to use both behaviors. While my writing and typing is Automatic, choosing what to write and what idea I wish to convey is being done with Aware Behavior.

The D.C.P teaches people how to access and use both behaviors. Initially, it can be a bit of a struggle to learn a new behavior. But eventually, that behavior becomes learned and can become automatic. The essence of the D.C.P. in regards to the bi-modal model of behavior is that we can learn to interrupt the Automatic and eventually we have a new behavior which is now Automatic, but also updated and desirable.

Harry can learn to interrupt and stop his screaming and yelling. By practicing some of the skills and techniques of the D.C.P. his "new" behavior will eventually become automatic and a moment before he begins to yell and scream he will stop himself and engage another behavior. One of the objectives of the D.C.P. is to learn how to access and use both modes of behavior. One might choose to intentionally go into Automatic behavior and later choose to go back into Intentional or "Aware".

There are several components to the training necessary in order to achieve the ability to choose and access either mode of behavior. These components include a strong sense of self, and understanding of feelings and how to change them, a knowledge of how distress affects behavior and how to reduce it and a basic understanding of how human behavior works. These components will be addressed later in this book under various chapters.

Long Term Memory

It would appear that all patterns of behavior are in one's long term memory. However, not every pattern is a *distress pattern*. It is clear, however that all of these inappropriate and outdated patterns are triggered by distress. In fact, the more intense the distress is, the earlier in life a pattern will be triggered. It is not unusual to see adults acting like children when they get distressed. What is happening at this point is that a distress pattern is running. Remember, that these patterns are automatic and the individual has very little awareness or flexibility while the pattern is running. Of course one is aware if one is yelling or screaming, but the behavior seems to occur automatically. However, with practice, the behavior pattern, which is triggered by distress can be interrupted and changed.

Much of what is stored in our long term memory is not only useful, but essential. These automatic behaviors allow us to function. The problem arises when one is triggered by distress and is either inappropriate or outdated and is NOT something that we really wish to do.

Some people have asked if the Bimodal model of behavior corresponds to the two halves of the brain. It's an interesting comparison, but there is no connection. What we do know is that once a memory gets recorded into long term memory, it is there forever, unless the brain gets damaged. Recall, may be another matter, but the knowledge is still there. It's like a computer that has information in it, but you may not be able to access it at a particular time. The distress pattern also functions like a computer program. Once it is activated, it runs. It is always activated by distress, which is why an emphasis in the D.C.P. is stress reduction.

With a computer, one can reset the machine and even remove certain programs and files if desired. With the brain, all memories are permanent once they get into long term memory. Once a behavior is learned and gets into long term memory, it remains there. If the behavior was in response to distress it can be triggered. Even behaviors we learned as children can be activated and will run. It is worth repeating that the more intense the distress, the earlier in one's life a behavior pattern will be triggered. So, the next you see an adult acting like a child, you'll know why that individual is acting that way.

It is futile to argue with someone when they are running a distressed pattern. If you were to confront someone who was acting like a child, and tell them that they were acting like a child, they would deny it. The best thing to do in a situation like this is to not engage with the person, because you will be fighting a behavior pattern and patterns as you'll discover are designed to be self-perpetuating. If you want to talk with that person and have an intelligent conversation, talk to them later, when they are not distressed.

Here's an example. When someone is really angry there is no point trying to talk with them or reason with them. They are apt to say or do things that they would never say or do if they weren't angry. Wait until they calm down, then, talk to them. But be careful, because they could easily become distressed again and flip back into the Automatic behavior. There is another thing that might happen that would only compound the situation. You might become distressed (angry or hurt) and go into your patterned behavior. If this happened there would be two people each running a distress pattern at each other. All they can do is do what they learned to do. Don't expect any civil, rational behavior to take place until both parties cool down. Such conversations can be interesting and amusing to watch as long as you are not a part of them. Oftentimes, when both parties have calmed down and are back in Intentional behavior, they may both feel remorseful and regret acting the way they did. Such an experience often provides the motivation to learn how to interrupt unwanted (distress) behavior patterns.

APPLICATION of the DESIGNED CHANGED PROCESS

Much of this book will go into detail explaining how to use the D.C.P. For now, however, I will provide a simple explanation. Let's take Harry as an example – the newspaper editor who yells and screams when he gets distressed. This behavior pattern is one he learned quite early in life and it continues to run today when Harry experiences a lot of stress.

18

If Harry were trained in the D.C.P. he would first develop a strong sense of self (ME). He'd also learn about feelings; what they are, what they do and how to manage them.

With the help of a trainer, Harry would actually enter the Automatic mode of behavior. He would accomplish this by having his trainer deliberate attempt to distress Harry. Most of us know how to get another person distressed. It is often referred to as "pushing your buttons". Children are especially skilled at doing this.

So, Harry gets angry or frustrated and starts to yell, but that behavior is interrupted. A skilled trainer can actually move Harry in and out of distress. When the distress becomes too intense, Harry can use a variety of techniques (which will be discussed in subsequent chapters) to lower his stress level. With the help of a trainer, Harry can learn how to interrupt this distress pattern. Sometimes all it takes is a word or a phrase. Once the distress pattern is interrupted, Harry must replace the old behavior with a new one and then practice it until it becomes "automatic".

Here is the sequence of events that Harry might use:

Harry begins from a place of strength by Celebrating his "ME". With the help of a trainer, Harry deliberately experiences some distress. If the distress becomes too intense and Harry can't focus on the directions he is receiving from the trainer, he uses a variety of techniques to lower his stress level. An interrupter is introduced – this could a word, a phrase or even an action in itself. This is practiced until Harry can do it himself. Then the old behavior is replaced by the new. This is also practiced repeatedly until Harry has mastered it.

The result is Harry gets distressed, but instead of yelling and screaming, he interrupts the old behavior and engages the new one. Once learned, all this happens in a matter of seconds. The ability to use both modes of behavior is essential. It has already been emphasized how useful "Automatic" behavior is. Yet, it has also been demonstrated that some old behaviors are inappropriate or out dated and are triggered by stress.

Intentional Behavior, which provides a maximum amount of awareness, flexibility and choice is far less efficient than Automatic Behavior. Yet, Intentional behavior is highly desirable when a creative solution is desired. Some people think that the goal of the D.C.P. is to only use Intentional Behavior. However, the real goal is to be able to use both and to be able to switch back and forth from one to the other. There are several other components that are necessary to learn in order to do this. Plus it requires practice

A number of people have asked if the D.C.P. is behavioral or humanistic. The answer is – it is both. It is behavioral in the sense that the new behavior must be repeated and practiced. However, it is also humanistic in regards to self esteem and feelings. Most behavioral approaches do not deal with feelings and often don't even acknowledge them. For example, in Exposure Therapy, a type of behavioral therapy, a client is gradually exposed to a situation that evokes fear or some other type of distress. Unfortunately, with this type of approach, the client may become too distressed to ever succeed in overcoming the fear, through the exposure process. It's all a matter of desensitization and gradually exposing the client to more and more of the item or situation that causing the distress. But the client can become so distressed that they terminate the therapy.

On the other hand, the D.C.P. is also behavioral in that a client learns a new behavior and must practice that new behavior in order to become skilled using it. This part of the D.C.P has some similarities to behavioral techniques.

20

However, in behavioral techniques, one would not expect to find any skills designed to enhance self esteem (ME) nor information about how to change feelings.

There are several aspects of the D.C.P that make it unique. In additional to it being comprised of both behavioral and humanistic techniques, the D.C.P. is both intriguing and fun. Once an individual has learned the key components, they find it both very interesting and enjoyable. Many of the techniques are instant and portable – meaning they can be done anywhere without any special equipment or conditions. People who study the D.C.P. become very adept at identifying distressed behavior patterns – their own and those of others. It becomes even more fun when people learn how to actually interrupt their own behavior pattern. There is a technique called the "Interrupter" which is known to produce hardy laughter. This will be discussed in another chapter.

It should be noted that D.C.P. is not considered therapy. Rather it is the teaching of specific skills and information.

Summary: Essentially the Bimodal model of human behavior consists of two different types of behavior: Intentional and Automatic. The D.C.P. teaches people how to use both modes of behavior. While the Automatic mode is rigid, repetitive and unaware, it is highly efficient and can be compared to a computer program. The Intentional mode is aware, flexible and provides a maximum of choice. Using the Intentional mode, one might actually choose to go into the Automatic mode of behavior. The difficulty is that once in the Automatic mode, it is quite difficult to access the Intentional mode. However, the D.C.P. actually provides a way to do this by building interruptions into the Automatic mode that would enable one to access the Intentional behavior.

One central component is a strong sense of self-esteem, known in the D.C.P. as "ME". It should be noted that a strong sense of self, is not the same as being selfish. This issue is addressed in a workshop entitled, "Celebrate ME", a self esteem enhancement workshop, which is available online (www.designedchange.org). "Celebrate ME" is discussed in Chapter Three.

In the next chapter I will discuss the difference between "Stress vs. Distress", which is a key component of the D.C.P.

Chapter 2 – Stress and Distress

A major component of the D.C.P. is the concept of "stress" and "distress". Stress is considered to be external – the forces that we experience everyday. Many people think of this as pressure or tension. Distress on the other hand is internal and Selye defines distress as "damaging or unpleasant stress", (Selye 1975, 11).

The concept of stress was initially used in engineering. A piece of metal could be stressed to a certain degree before it would break. Engineers developed formulas for testing the strength of various pieces of metal.

Eventually, the concept of stress was applied to people. They could only tolerate so much stress before they began to feel uncomfortable.

It's interesting to note that what is stressful to one person, may actually be a source of pleasure to someone else. For example, some people really enjoy riding on a roller coaster, while others who get queasy riding in an elevator would find a roller coaster ride to be very distressing.

Stress vs. Distress

Most people do not distinguish between stress and distress. For most people, when they are talking about "stress", they actually mean "distress". As soon as you begin to feel uncomfortable, you are experiencing distress. To a degree "stress" can be motivating. But too much stress results in distress. For example, if you have a project to complete by a certain time, a little bit of stress can motivate you to get it done. But if you wait until the night before the project is due, you will most likely experience distress and will feel so pressured to get the project done that you might feel overwhelmed and quite upset – which will only contribute to more distress and inhibit you from getting the project done.

The Stress Response

Many books have been written about the Stress Response. Essentially what happens is when we perceive a threat our brain releases various chemicals that help prepare the body. The blood is moved to the vital organs.

The important thing to remember is that any threat, real or imaginary can trigger this response. If you perceive something as a threat, then it is real to you and your body reacts to the distress (uncomfortable feeling).

Much has been written about stress and stress management. A key point to remember is that distress is largely a perception of a threat. It makes no difference to us whether the threat is real or not. It is real to our brains and our bodies respond to various chemicals that are released once a threat is perceived.

Effect of Stress on the Human Body

The following information is not exclusively part of the D.C.P. It is provided, however, to demonstrate the profound effects of stress upon the human body.

The part of the brain that first detects stress and "sounds the alarm" is called the hippocampus. The reticular activating system is a part of the brain that sends signals to various areas of the brain. When we experience stress the hypothalamus of the brain activates the *endocrine system* and the *automatic nervous system*. A chemical called *corticotrophin releasing factor* (CRF) is released by the hypothalamus, which causes the pituitary gland to secrete *adrenocorticotropic hormone* (ACTH). This is a powerful chemical that causes the adrenal cortex to release corticoid hormones. Glucocorticoids mainly affect the metabolism of carbohydrates and they are considered steroids. Cortisol in particular has been identified as a "stress hormone" that affect metabolism (Greenberg 1996).

In addition, the hypothalamus also stimulates the thyroid and the pituitary gland which secrete oxytocin and vasopressin (ADH). Vasopressin (1) is an antidiuretic hormone that reduces the loss of water in urine. A diuretic has the opposite effect. [1]

The Endocrine System

The Endocrine System includes all of the following glands: pituitary, thyroid, parathyroid and adrenal glands as well as the pancreas, ovaries, testes, pineal gland and thymus gland. (Greenberg p. 18). (It is worth noting that an under active thyroid can produce a host of physical and psychological symptoms including cognitive issues, depression, brittle nails and dry skin, to name just of few of them). These glands secrete hormones. Many of these hormones have a profound affect on various body parts. Cortisol, which has been previously mentioned, is responsible for the "fight or flight" syndrome. It increases blood sugar which provides us with more energy. It also increases arterial blood pressure. All of this is designed to help us fight or run from the stressor. Cortisol also decreases lymphocytes that help destroy invading substances, like bacteria. Therefore, an increase in cortisol decreases our immune system and makes us more susceptible to illness.

Aldosterone is another hormone that has a major impact upon the body. It increases blood pressure to transport food and oxygen to various active parts of the body. The result is a decrease in urine production and an increase in sodium retention. This is why many people with high blood pressure are told to reduce or eliminate salt from their diet.

You can begin to see how stress affects various parts of our body in plays a role in many illnesses.

[1] Colorado State University. Antidiuretic Hormone Vasopressin http://www.vivo.colostate.edu/hbooks/pathphys/endoc rine/hypopit/adh.html

The Nervous System

The nervous system consists of the sympathetic and parasympathetic nervous system. When you get stressed here are just some of the changes that take place in your body: increased heart rate and increased force when the heart contracts, coronary arteries dilate, pupils dilate, most bodily functions speed up (basal metabolic rate), blood vessels in the muscles and skin of the arms and legs constrict. (This is not a complete list of all that happens as a result of stress upon the nervous system).

Most people have heard of the chemical adrenalin (epinephrine) and some have heard of noradrenalin (norepinephrine). Both of these are hormones but each acts differently and controls different parts of the body. Noradrenalin is both a neurotransmitter and a stress hormone. It plays a major role in the "fight or flight" syndrome. Adrenalin also is a neurotransmitter and plays a role in the "fight or flight" syndrome. A simplified way of explain the two is that Adrenalin causes the heart rate to increase while noradrenalin reduces heart rate.

The Cardiovascular System

This system keeps the blood circulated and is significantly affected by stress. Stress causes blood vessels to contract, increases blood volume, and increases blood pressure. Also, the heart is affected by stress. The force of its contraction increases. In addition serum cholesterol levels increase as well. This increases the possibility of clogging the arteries and can result in a heart attack. Severe stress can shock the heart "to such an extent that sudden death occurs" (Greenberg, 1996 25)

The Gastrointestinal System

Stress has a very significant effect upon the gastrointestinal (GI) system. Here is what happens. Saliva is decreased and there may be uncontrollable contractions in the muscles of the esophagus. Swallowing may be difficult. The amount of hydrochloric acid in the stomach increases, which can cause all sorts of digestive problems, including an upset stomach, indigestion, even vomiting. Also stress can result in diarrhea or the opposite problem – constipation.

All Body Parts

If it appears to you that stress can affect every part of the body, you are correct. Stress can affect muscles, too. Muscle tension is real! Muscles can become tensed, tight and start to ache. Stress can even affect your skin. Certain types of hives and rashes and other types of skin eruptions are stress related. In addition, stress can cause your skin to feel cold, clammy and cause you to look pale.

In summary, stress had a profound affect upon the human body. It is imperative to learn how to manage stress. The D.C.P. offers numerous ways to manage stress via cognitive, affective and behavioral techniques. The specific ways of changing one's feelings as a way of managing stress is a unique approach which has not been duplicated by other disciplines and strategies. The specific ways of changing feelings will be discussed in the chapter on Feelings.

Distress causes three things to happen.

1. Distress Distorts perception
2. Distress impairs thinking
3. Distress triggers automatic behaviors (habits)

Distress Distorts Perception

Police have documented that distress distorts perception. Many times they will interview a group of witnesses and each witness will give different account of what took place or a different description of the suspect's appearance. Other examples of distress distorting perception have occurred when people were upset or angry – often perceiving events differently than if they had been calm and relaxed.

Consider this scenario – You are walking down a street in an unfamiliar part of town. It's dusk and suddenly you see a man approaching you with a big stick. There is no one else around. Many people would perceive this individual approaching with a big stick to be a threat.

There are many other situations when people become distressed.

Consider this 2nd scenario – Beth walks into her office and her co-worker says to her, "the boss wants to see you, now!" Beth becomes distressed immediately and begins to think that she must have done something wrong.

Here's another example: Alice, a high school student, who isn't very popular, answered a question wrong in one of her classes. The entire class laughed at her. After class, one student even said to her, "Why do you even bother to answer questions? Everyone knows that you're dumb". Walking home from school that day, Alice saw some of her classmates from that class walking on the other side of the street. They were laughing and Alice perceived that they were laughing at her. In fact, they didn't even see Alice on the other side of the street and weren't even talking about her.

Can you recall a time when your perception of what happened was distorted by distress?

Distress Impairs Thinking

Perception is not the only thing affected by distress. Distress impairs thinking.

Most students have personally experienced how distress impairs thinking. They've studied for a test. Yet, when they actually take the test, they can't think due to nervousness or pressure. Often in times of crisis, people don't think. Instead, they just react. This is what happened many years ago at the Three Mile Island Nuclear facility. Because workers reacted as they had been trained to do, rather than question if the gauges were accurate or if some other action was necessary, they nearly caused a meltdown of the core of the reactor.

Oftentimes, when people are under pressure (distressed), they can't think. If you've ever watched any TV quiz shows, you have probably witnessed this.

Speaking of witnesses, sometimes witnesses get confused under cross examination in court. Or, if you've ever been in an automobile accident and filed a lawsuit, you can be deposed. The opposing attorney can ask you all sorts of questions and you are required to answer them. A deposition doesn't take place in a courtroom. It usually takes place in a law office. The fact is, when you get distressed it becomes difficult to think.

Job interviews are another source of distress for many people. At stake is a job or even your career. It can be difficult to think and give a good answer when you know that everything you say and do is being evaluated. Job interviews can be distressing. However, with practice one can learn how to do well on them.

Perhaps you can recall a time when you were distressed and were unable to think.

Distress Triggers Automatic Behavior (habits)

Distress can trigger an automatic behavior (a habit). Ever watch two adults arguing? Oftentimes they seem like they are acting like children. They automatically resort to earlier learned behaviors.

Each year, people who live in New England have to drive on snow and ice. If they hit the brakes when they are on snow or ice, they will go into a skid. Yet, people panic (feel distressed), and they hit the brakes and the car begins to skid instead of stopping. So, they hit the brakes even harder, causing the car to skid even more – sometimes going completely out of control.

Sometimes, discovering your own automatic behavior can be difficult to do. However, other people will have little difficulty identifying something you do automatically. What I'm really talking about are habits. Not all habits are triggered by distress. But those that are can be very inappropriate.

The effects of distress can be disastrous depending upon the circumstances. In summary,

Distress distorts perception, impairs thinking and triggers automatic responses (habits). These responses don't necessarily happen in the order given.

Effects of Stress Often Underestimated

The effects of stress upon the human body are often underestimated. Many people don't realize how stress can affect the physical body as well as the mind. Distress can affect nearly every system in the body. The cardiovascular system is often affected with an increase in heart rate and blood pressure. The digestive system can be affected with indigestion, upset stomach or the need to go to the bathroom. The nervous system is affected in many complex ways often resulting in the release of stress hormones that can trigger all sorts of responses. The actual response is determined in part by the type of distress. For example, fear causes the blood in the circulatory system to move to protect the vital organs resulting in fingers and toes getting cold. A "cold sweat" is often the result of fear as well, as the body responds to the distress. There are many other physical changes that result from distress and they are well beyond the scope and nature of this book. Many illnesses are aggravated if not caused by distress.

The effect of stress on the mind is another area that deserves discussion. There is a connection between the mind and the body. Thinking certain distressing thoughts can result in physical changes in the body. Anxiety for some people is especially disruptive and can cause a host of physical symptoms including raising heart rate and blood pressure, cause difficulty in breathing, result in nervousness, shaking and trembling, heart palpitations and can also affect cognitive functions (thinking and Executive Functions). Many people have ended up in the emergency room of a hospital thinking they were having a heart attack and discover it was anxiety. Some of the symptoms are very similar and it can be difficult for an individual who is not medically trained to tell the difference.

Earlier definitions of stress included the "wear and tear" on the body. Everyone has a certain part of their body that is prone to stress and more likely to break down. Do you know people who always seem to get stomachaches and also experience fear? Do you know people who are lonely and repeatedly get sore throats?

People with a lot of anger frequently get chest pains. While this is anecdotal evidence, we do know that stress (more accurately "distress"), raises havoc with people's health. Stress is a contributing factor to many illnesses and conditions and makes the condition worse. In some instances, stress is the cause of specific illnesses and conditions.

For many people stress plays a significant role in blood pressure. Blood pressure can change in an instant and lots of things can affect it, including how you feel emotionally and what you are thinking. A common condition that many people have is called *White Coat Syndrome* where people become very anxious when they have their blood pressure taken, because oftentimes the person taking the reading is dressed in white. The reading is high in the doctor's office, but returns to normal when they go home. While doctors allow for this when they take a reading, some people have extreme *White Coat Syndrome* and become extremely anxious or nervous resulting in a much higher reading.

While Hypertension (High Blood Pressure) is a serious condition, sometimes primary care physicians overreact and insist on putting a patient on medication. Most physicians don't have time to talk to their patients about life style changes and many patients are seeking a quick fix anyway and welcome a pill as oppose to making a lifestyle change.

Stress is pervasive throughout our society. It's an accepted way of living in the 21st century. The D.C.P. offers numerous ways of reducing stress and managing it. These techniques are practical, effective and enjoyable and will be discussed in the Chapter about Feelings.

Stress and Decision Making

The impact of stress upon decision making is also considerable.

If you have an important decision to make (which can be stressful in itself), you would be well advised to get yourself into a calm, relaxing state of mind before making the decision. The D.C.P. offers numerous ways of doing this and many of these methods will be discussed in the forthcoming chapters, especially, "Celebrate ME" and "Feelings". However, many people make a decision when they are distressed and sometimes make the wrong decision. This further complicates their life and increases their stress level. Such decisions as whether to accept a job offer and move to another location are important decisions. Change of any type creates stress. But if you make the wrong change, you compound the stress. Even a good change can be stressful.

Bill is a sales manager and recently was offered a promotion. His new job would give him much more responsibility and he'd have to work with a bunch of new people. He'd get a substantial increase in salary, but also a substantial increase in stress. Is it worth it? This is a question that each person has to answer for themselves. A factor to consider is how well Bill handles change and particularly, stress. It should be noted that what is stressful for one person can actually be source of pleasure for someone else. So, while some people might find it stressful and challenging to have to make new relationships with various employees, other people would enjoy doing that. Another example is public speaking. This is something I personally really enjoy. Yet, I know of several people who would feel terrified to have to speak before a group of people. I once taught an undergraduate course where some students told me that they'd rather get an "F" than stand up in front of the class and give an oral presentation.

(I allowed those students to submit a detailed written report).

Stress is a Perception

As has already been stated, stress is largely a perception. If you perceive something as stressful, then it is to you. Our brains have great difficulty distinguishing between an actual threatening event and the perception of one. In addition, because we can visualize or imagine (most people can), we are able to ask ourselves the "What if" questions and imagine something that hasn't happened? What if Bill accepts the new position and can't handle it? Asking "what if" questions is not necessarily a bad thing to do. It can help us create a contingency plan. But it can also paint a very distressing situation of probable outcomes that we wouldn't want to happen. It requires a low stress level and a clear mind to properly assess these situations. Yet, most of us make a decision when we are stressed, rather than when we are relaxed. If you perceive that something is stressful, then it is to you. If you perceive that something is enjoyable, then that is also true. Perhaps this explains somewhat why there are people who like to engage in dangerous activities such as sky diving, hang gliding, jumping off a high cliff into a river. They are often called thrill seekers, but many of these people don't see these activities as stressful. Yet ask them to stand in front of a room and give a talk and many of them would freeze up and not be able to do it. This demonstrates the highly personalized way that stress affects us. If you view something as stressful, then it is to you.

Besides asking "What if" questions, may of us can visualize an event that hasn't happened. A young man asking a woman out on a date may visualize her rejecting him. So, he decides not to ask her out. We human beings have the ability to visualize and imagine what might actually happen before it happens and it might not happen at all! While this can be a highly creative and useful skill, it can also be a continuous source of stress. Again, there are specific therapies that deal with these issues, however the client must be able to reduce his or her stress level in order us use specific techniques from these therapies.

The emphasis with the D.C.P. is one of teaching skills to reduce stress, improve one's sense of self esteem and interrupt unwanted behavior patterns.

Many young children find taking a bath to be stressful, while many adults find such an activity to be very relaxing. But to a young child who hears the sound of water being sucked down the drain may perceive that he might be sucked down the drain as well. The noise itself is stressful to many young children. Some children also get stressed about taking a shower. They can't seem to adjust the flow of water and regulate the temperature. All it takes is for a child to get soap in his or her eyes while taking a shower and it won't be an experience that they will want to repeat. Mention taking a shower to them and they perceive their eyes burning and stinging from the soap.

As you can see, stress is very pervasive and highly individualized. As our culture and society continues to become more complex, there is a growing need to learn how to reduce stress and manage it. There is also a need to anchor oneself, to know and trust that there is one person you can depend upon – yourself. This idea is developed in the chapter on Celebrate ME.

The D.C.P. does not recommend escapist strategies. There is stress everywhere. It is largely a perception and a matter of learning how to deal with it. Distraction or avoidance techniques can temporarily give one a break. But when you return the stress is still there. Some people think they'd have less stress if they moved to the suburbs or even rural areas. Living in a city is often noisy, crowded, polluted and can be a high crime area. But people who live in the suburbs also have their problems. Public transportation can be nonexistent. If your car dies, there aren't any buses or other methods of public transportation. If you live in rural area, your nearest neighbor might literally be a few miles away. If you need city services, like police or the fire department, you will probably have to wait a lot longer for someone to assist you.

Rather than attempting to escape from stress or temporarily distract yourself, the D.C.P. recommends learning specific techniques to reduce distress and manage feelings. There are some other disciplines that advocate analyzing a thought/perception to determine if it is accurate or not. This is definitely a valuable skill. However, as has already been discussed, Distress Distorts Perception, Impairs Thinking and Triggers Automatic Responses. So, in order to analyze if the perceived threat is real, you would still need to manage stress by reducing it and lowering your stress level.

The issue of stress is further compounded in several ways. First, recall that stress triggers automatic responses. Also recall that once in Automatic Behavior, one has very little awareness. I've met several people who weren't even aware that they were stressed! Another complication is the fact that change is taking place at a faster rate than has ever been recorded before. A lot of this has to do with technology, the Internet, high speed connections, Smart Phones and other technological devices. While these devices help us to do things much faster than ever before, they also create stress for a lot of people. Sometimes people respond too quickly. It's easy if you're upset to fire off an email. But without carefully thinking about what you say, you might be compounding the issue or introducing new issues into an already messy situation.

The time to make important decisions is when you are relaxed and not in distress. The ability to lower one's stress level and manage feelings is essential. While there are many different types of stress management techniques, there are basically two different approaches: proactive and reactive. The D.C.P. teaches both, but encourages and teachers participants to become proactive in managing stress. An emphasis is placed upon how stress affects behavior.

While it has been mentioned several times it is worth repeating again that Distress Distorts Perception, Impairs Thinking and Triggers Automatic Responses (habits). It is essential to have a strong sense of self (ME) and learn how to reduce and manage stress. While distress has a profound affect upon our bodies, it also has a profound affect upon our minds. The fact is people can not think clearly if they are distressed and if the distress intensifies, they will revert back to an earlier learned behavior pattern, resulting in rigid behavior, which may appear to be childlike.

When important, intelligent decisions need to be made, it is imperative to reduce the intensity of distress. Otherwise, a poor decision is likely, which often creates a negative response, resulting in more distress, requiring yet another decision, etc. This produces a negative cycle and is likely to get the individual or group or business in more and more difficulty – which in turn increases the stress level. The way out of this cycle is to reduce the distress, strengthen one's sense of self (ME) and then make a decision when one is in a non-distressed state.

The Feelings Workshop includes stress management in addition to specific information about what feelings are, what they do and most importantly, how one can change them.

There are many different ways of managing stress.

Here is a list of some of the different ways of managing stress:

- Escape – attempting to run away from the stress, if only for a brief period of time

- Affective – changing feelings *

- Avoidance- not engaging in situations that are stress producing

- Relaxation- a system of stressing and relaxing muscles

- Meditation – disciplining the mind by developing the ability to focus. There a many different types of meditation and various techniques

- Exercise- physical exercise, which is recommended for everyone

- Visualization – the ability to see images. Many guided visualizations are available.

- Breathing – specific techniques to reduce stress

- Cognitive (working with thoughts, changing them, interrupting them)*

- Behavioral – interrupting a behavior pattern and replacing it with a new one and practicing that new behavior*

- OTC medications – various medications one can buy without a prescription

- Rx – prescription medications, requiring a doctor's order

- Not included – many other therapies or programs that require you to work with a trained professional such as a therapist, massage therapist, hypnotist, NLP Practitioner, etc.

- The D.C.P. primarily uses cognitive, affective and behavioral techniques to manage stress.

A central part of the D.C.P. is a solid sense of self (ME) which will be discussed in the next chapter. A solid sense of self (ME) is essential in understanding and using the D.C.P.

Here are some exercises regarding Distress.

1. Distress distorts perception. Note a time your perception was distorted.

2. Distress impairs thinking. Note a time that your thinking was impaired.

Distress triggers automatic behaviors (habits). Note an automatic behavior you use when distressed.

Note any difficulty you had doing this exercise. What feeling did you experience? Was it distressing? (Recall distress is any uncomfortable feeling.)

---

[1] Colorado State University. Antidiuretic Hormone Vasopressin
http://www.vivo.colostate.edu/hbooks/pathphys/endocrine/hypopit/adh.html

Chapter 3 – Celebrate ME

A central part of the Designed Change Process is having a solid, positive sense of one's self image or self esteem. The Celebrate ME workshop is designed to do this and provides participants with a number of portable skills that can be used anytime and any place.

Exactly what is meant by the term "ME"? The best description that I can give is a solid sense of who you are, the many positive qualities that you have and what capabilities you have. The actual term "Celebrate ME" was never defined in the original materials created and developed by Sargent for the D.C.P. Sargent had this to say about "ME":

> *At the center of all the change that is upon us is the individual. Deep at the heart is my ME. My ME gets buffeted by my old patterns as I find myself doing things that are against them. It gets buffeted by others around me as I do things different from what they would have me do. My ME is pushed first one way, then the other.*

[From Tom Sargent's Training Manual. ND. 1]

The Celebrate ME workshop is a self esteem enhancement training program providing participants with gentle techniques to appreciate themselves. A significant distinction is made between appreciating oneself and bragging. Upon careful analysis, it is often discovered that the person who is bragging actually lacks self esteem and is emphasizing one trait to cover up an inferior one. The training consists of information, experiential exercises and skills development. The first half of each training session is structured with mini-presentations, exercises and learning activities and some sharing of what people experience during an exercise. The second half of each session consists of skills development and discussion.

A Catalog of Celebrations

Throughout the entire training program, participants are taught the concept of "celebration" – to genuinely appreciate who they are, what they feel and various patterns that they use. Here is a brief description of some of the techniques that are used:

1. New and Good – participants are asked to identify something that they recently experienced that was "good". "Our minds work by association, and if we can remember one good thing the good feeling will come along with it. As experience goes on the individual learns to celebrate more and more good experience."(Sargent 1974, p18).

2. Scanning – participants recall all the times they have felt a certain feeling, such as excited, happy or peaceful. Any feeling can be scanned, even distressed feelings. Scanning distress feelings can be useful because the process leads to discovering how we actually use distress and how it connects to patterns of behavior.

3. Random Pleasant Memories – are memories of different types of enjoyable feelings associated with various experiences. This technique works best with another person who calls out various types of events such as relaxing under a tree, a parade, a puppy, sitting by a fire, a refreshing drink, etc. This technique is very relaxing and has been know to help headaches go away.

4. Good Qualities – are anything about oneself that is positive. This is the central activity for celebrating my ME. Many people find this difficult to do and claim that this is bragging. It isn't. Taking time to genuinely appreciate oneself is NOT bragging. People who brag are actually

insecure about some aspect of themselves, so they emphasize (brag) about some other aspect to direct attention away from their insecurity.

As you celebrate your ME you may find yourself qualifying each good quality. For example you might say, "I'm punctual *sometimes*. The word *sometimes* is a qualifier. Qualifiers aren't allowed. Often people will find a number of ways to qualify their good qualities by using such phrases as "I'm sort of ..." or "I guess I'm ...." Again, qualifiers aren't allowed. The participants are asked to repeat the validation without any qualifiers. There are additional techniques for helping people who have difficulty eliminating the qualifiers. They are asked to pick a validation that they really believe is true and then scan all the ways that this is true. For example, if a participant says, "I'm a kind person, usually", they would be asked to scan all the ways that they are kind and then repeat the validation without the qualifier.

Another sneaky way around celebrating your ME is to refer to your role or function. For example, someone might say, I'm a good mother, or I'm a good worker. In each case they would be asked to celebrate the qualities that make them a good mother or worker. Celebration of Me is a central activity and one that requires practice and repetition. Once mastered, it becomes a real source of strength.

6. My Limits – helps participants become clear about what limits they have and how they impact upon what they do or don't do. Consider this scenario – when I'm angry I won't share anything with you. Then, when I feel guilty, I give you everything, even something that I need. First, I go past my limit in order to express my anger. Then I let you walk all over me- past my unseen limits again. I have lost something very important – my ME, my sense of self, my appreciation of my good qualities. Now, to get

42

your love or approval I allow you to exceed my limits and I lose more of my sense of ME. So, participants are asked to celebrate their ME and their limits.

7. Differences – are things that we usually hide from each other. We tend to fear people that are different from us. However, the differences are what really enhance our lives. Imagine if we were all the same. Imagine if we all wore the same type and color clothing and all did the same things, ate the same food. What a boring world we'd have. One of the greatest things we have to offer each other are our differences. We have different skills and interests and different experiences have shaped our values and behavior.

Instead of hiding our differences, the D.C.P. encourages people to celebrate their differences as part of their ME.

7. Sexuality –is one of the differences that we hide the most. Despite much more liberal thinking regarding sexual differences than previous decades, it can still be dangerous in certain situations to be different sexually. What exactly is different? That depends upon who you ask and most people will tell you – don't ask! It is not a coincidence that the military has a "don't ask, don't tell" policy.

Sexuality is something that can be celebrated as well. Many people are embarrassed to say that they are sexual or to describe some other aspect of their sexuality. This is yet another aspect of the celebration of ME.

8. Favorite Patterns – are patterns of behavior that are usually triggered by distress. These patterns worked well in the past but have become outdated and inappropriate. Now they interfere with our intelligence and what we want to do. Ever run an old program on a computer? You try and get the computer to do something, but the program won't allow it. Our patterns of behavior are

similar. But, by celebrating our favorite patterns we mock them and make fun of them and can lessen their effect. Participants can also celebrate this pattern and appreciate how good we do them. This may seem strange at first. But we all have behavior patterns and we run them extremely well. So why not appreciate how well you run a pattern. Patterns are rigid, repetitive and automatic, so they are easy to recognize and others can recognize them quite easily. Consider these scenarios – Harry gets angry and stomps out of the room. Beth gets angry and starts crying. These behaviors happen automatically with enough distress. Celebrate them!

9. Down Feelings – are distress feelings that don't feel "good". Feelings of any particular type bring about more of the same feelings. They intensify by focusing on them. Whatever you focus on will intensify. It's the same process used for celebrating good feelings. Focus on depression and you can get depressed about the fact that you are depressed. Now you have two depressions! However, if you celebrate how good you are at being depressed, your mood will lighten. You might even chuckle because it seems like such a ridiculous thing to do. You can take any distressing feeling and celebrate how good you are at doing it. Maybe you could get some business cards printed and give lessons in how to be depressed or angry or whatever down feeling you experience. Does this sound silly and ridiculous? Well, it is. The really strange thing is once you start celebrating your down feeling they lessen and go away, especially when combined with other techniques.

10. *I like How I Feel* ____ *When I* ____. This is a great way to identify pleasant feelings and the association with each feeling. First identify a pleasant feeling that you enjoy. Then identify when you get it. For example, I like how I feel energetic when I dance. Or, I like how I feel

strong when I lift weights. You can choose any feeling, but you can't use the word "good" for a feeling. It's important to identify what a good feeling is.

Some people find it helpful to reverse the sentence and first identify what they like to do and then identify the feelings. For example, when I dance I feel energetic. Or, when I lift weights, I feel strong.

By celebrating your ME you can develop a solid sense of self that no one can take away from you. In addition to these techniques, Sargent created a special visualization called "Special Place". This was a guided imagery. But it wasn't designed to just escape from stress. It was designed to be used in the mist of distress. The guided imagery contained built in associations, so it could be recalled with a single word or phrase.

The most remarkable use of this took place during one of the Celebrate ME workshops where a participant demonstrated such mastery of it that he was able to experience being called names and have insults thrown at him and just hear it as noise. He had developed such a strong sense of ME that he simply dismissed the name calling and insults as "noise", instead of getting angry or annoyed.

This demonstrates the power of this technique and the practical aspect. Imagine being attacked verbally and not automatically responding with anger or hostility. If children learned how to do this, bullying would probably fade away. A bully can't have any fun if he can't get a victim distressed. There are many other applications and implications of this technique that could be the basis of another book.

Rationale and Explanation of Various Techniques

New and Good Technique – While this is simple technique to teach or to use, it is more complicated to explain how it works. The technique requires that an individual focus on something that is non-distressing (pleasurable). But this is much more than just a technique of focusing upon something pleasurable. The technique is based on the fact that distress distorts perception, impairs thinking and triggers automatic behaviors (habits). When you get distressed you can't think. Therefore, it becomes essential to move out of the distress and this technique forces you to do that. By focusing on something that is pleasurable or non- distressing, the intensity of the distress (feeling) is actually reduced. Once the intensity of the feeling subsides, access to the Intentional mode of behavior is available. It's important not to focus too long on any specific New and Good experience, because if you focus on something long enough, you can find something that isn't so good about it.

It is important when giving instructions on how to do this technique that the word "think" is not used. Rather, than asking someone to think of a New and Good experience, it is far more effective to ask someone to identify a New and Good experience. If some can't identify a New and Good experience, then they are asked to recall an "Old and Good" experience. In rare instances when people are so distressed that they can't even recall an "Old and Good" experience, they are asked, "What's the least bad thing that has happened to you lately?" This will usually produce a chuckle and enable them to at least recall an Old and Good experience.

Portability – What makes this technique so useful is that it literally can be done anywhere, especially when on is waiting, such as waiting in a waiting room of a doctor's office, or stuck in traffic or waiting for a light to change. It is also a great way to begin a meeting or a family meal. The technique can be done silently to oneself, or shared with others and can also be written down in a journal or diary.

Pain vs. Pleasure – Ultimately pain and pleasure are incompatible. The stronger one will win. The rationale for using this technique is to force your brain to focus on something that is pleasant rather than continuing to focus on something that is unpleasant (distressing). The fact is there is always something that is "New and Good", but when we are distressed it's like having tunnel vision or wearing dark sunglasses. We're not able to see anything that is good. (Recall that perception is distorted when distressed). Usually once a person identifies one New and Good, they will be able to identify others. There is a tendency to keep focusing upon distress that only makes it seem worse. This is also called ruminating. Conversely, the opposite happens when we focus on something that is New and Good. We find other New and Goods as well.

Scanning – is a versatile technique and there are different things that one could scan. To do scanning, one simply focuses on a specific topic and recalls all the times, places or ways they have experience a particular feeling. For example, if you were to scan joy, you would briefly identify all the times or places or ways that you've experienced joy. It's important to be brief and move fairly rapidly from one memory to the next. A good analogy is skimming the cream off a cup of coffee. If you go too deep, you'll get the coffee as well. In fact, I sometimes called the Scanning technique the "Skimming" technique.

Scanning Distress – While scanning is used mostly to find pleasant feelings it can be useful to scan for a distress feeling. Using the D.C.P. people are taught to access different feelings in order to access either mode of behavior (Intentional vs. Automatic). In order to gain understanding of a distressed pattern, it can be useful and sometimes necessary to scan a specific distressed feeling state to see how it connects with a pattern. This is usually done with the help of another person, trained in the D.C.P.

Scanning Specific Topics - Sometimes it can be useful to scan a specific topic, especially if one has difficulty with a particular feeling. For example, you could scan all the times that you accomplished something. This would be an excellent way to bolster self esteem. Another application of this technique would be to scan all of the skills you use for a job. This might be an excellent use of this technique if you are writing a new resume and/or applying for a position.

Multiple Scanning - Different types of feelings can be scanned. Often in training programs, D.C.P. participants will be asked to scan a pleasant feeling such as joy for a minute. Then they would be asked to scan anger for a minute and finally scan times they've felt peaceful for another minute. If one were seeking a job, it would be useful to scan the various skills that you possess, and how you're competent and ways you feel confident.

Good Qualities – The ability to appreciate (and celebrate) the good qualities you have is an essential part of the D.C.P. It is important to note the distinction between appreciating oneself vs. bragging. To take time to genuinely appreciate your good qualities is quite different from bragging. In fact, people who brag usually do so to cover up or defect attention from areas in their live where they feel inferior. The appreciating of one's good qualities is called "celebration of self" and there are a variety of ways to do this. Sometimes one could scan "ways I'm special" or "my good qualities. Another way to do this would be to scan "my accomplishments".

Enjoyable Activities is a specific technique that I have created and it is done by making a list of 12 enjoyable activities on a piece of paper. Next to each activity that you have selected, identify the strength, skill or talent you use to do that activity. There will either be a strength, a skill or a talent, but not necessarily all three. But each activity you

48

do uses at least one of these qualities. For example, I like to plant a garden. I do use physical strength to do this in terms of turning over the soil, using a rake and other hand tools. The skill I use is my knowledge of what to plant and where.

Another example would be composing music. Here, I use several skills, such as my ability to read and write music. The talent I use is putting various notes together and producing a melody and harmonizing it.

After you have listed each strength, skill or talent, the next step is to take each quality and complete this sentence, "I like how I'm _____. In the blank, you list the actually strength, skill or talent. You do this for each strength, skill or talent.

The last part of this activity is to complete this sentence, "I'm _____. In the blank, you put the actual strength, skill or talent. There are variations on a theme here and if you wanted to make this more challenging, you could say each sentence in front of a mirror.

Rationale – The Enjoyable Activities technique provides a gentle way of bolstering self esteem. If you were to ask someone to tell you how they are "special", they would probably have a very difficult time doing so, unless they've had some training with the D.C.P. However, ask them to identify something they enjoy doing and they will easily be able to do that. The next step is slightly more challenging, but most people are able to identify what strength skill or talent they use to do that activity once they are given an example.

Differences –. Differences are things that we usually hide from each other. We tend to fear people that are different from us. However, the differences are what really enhance our lives. Imagine if we were all the same. Imagine if we all wore the same type and color of clothing and all did the same things, ate the same food. What a boring world we'd have. One of the greatest things we have to offer each other are our differences. We have different skills and interests and different experiences have shaped our values and behavior. Rather than hiding our differences, the D.C.P. encourages people to celebrate their differences as part of their ME.

Let's celebrate our differences. Instead of hiding them, let us appreciate them. Celebrating differences doesn't mean that you must do as I do or that I must do as you do. It simply means appreciating how we are different. It's like going into a bakery and instead of just one cake, there are several cakes: chocolate, yellow, some with cream, some with jelly, even an upside down cake. There are all sorts of differences and these differences make our lives more rich and interesting. Let's celebrate our differences and appreciate them, rather than hide them. Once you've developed a strong ME, differences are appreciated, rather than feared or hidden.

Down Feelings – The celebration of down feelings may seem like a strange thing to do. Why would someone want to celebrate their "down feelings"? Celebrating "down feelings" is a way of appreciating oneself. How good are you at being depressed or angry or sad? This may seem like a ridiculous thing to do. However, it does have merit. Once you begin to recognize how well you do depression or whatever distress feeling you experience (and maintain), you can begin to appreciate and celebrate that. Participants are encouraged to think of several ways of celebrating how good they are at a particular down feeling. Maybe you could teach a course "how to be angry" or get some business cards printed or even write a book about it. Does this sound silly, even ridiculous? Well, it is in a way. But the silliness is what defuses the intensity of the feeling.

Mocking "Down Feelings" is another way to diffuse their intensity. When you make fun of a distress feeling, it begins to weaken them. Down feelings like to be taken seriously and usually are, until you begin to mock them and make fun of them. This can easily be done by saying such things as "oh, my depression is so wonderful to have around" or "I'm getting angry – oh goodie!" It is the silliness that weakens the intensity of the down feeling.

Distress Patterns – Similar to celebrating "down feelings", you can celebrate distress patterns. These are patterns of behavior that are triggered by distress. The behavior pattern includes not only the distress feeling but also the behavior or activity that one does when experiencing this behavior. Just as you can celebrate (appreciate) how good you are at having a particular feeling, you can also celebrate how good you are at running a particular pattern. It is like watching an old movie. You know what will happen, because you've seen it before. Patterns, like distress feelings can be diffused by celebrating them. By focusing on the distress feeling, you can bring up the distress pattern. Usually this is done with the help of a trained individual. Once you begin focusing on a specific distress feeling, (example, anger), you will begin to do whatever you do when you are angry. For many people this involves, yelling or shouting, sometimes making a fist, literally feeling hot. Quite interesting, many women, who have been taught to not be angry, suppress the anger. Their backs will be hot, but their hands will be cold. Remember that behavior patterns are rigid and repetitive and often occur automatically. So, it's quite easy to run one. Once it is running, you can then celebrate it.

Mocking Patterns - just like feelings can be mocked. When you start making fun of one of your behavior patterns you are likely to weaken it just as you can weaken a distress feeling by mocking it as well. This technique is best done with someone who has been trained in the D.C.P.

Special Place – is a carefully constructed guided imagery. There are actually a few versions of this ranging from a simple "Special Place" to a more enhanced one with built in associations. The associations are feelings, visual images and good qualities of oneself. Once a person recalls just one, they get the entire experience and all the built in associations. It should be noted that this is quite different than the usual guided imagery, which while oftentimes quite pleasant and relaxing, doesn't have any specific associations. When it's over, it is over and the person needs to keep repeating the experience. Some people use a recording and keep listening to the recording. However the D.C.P. provides several ways for people to recall their "Special Place" with the built in associations.

The Special Place is not meant to be an escapist technique. Instead, participants are taught how to access their Special Place and be very present and respond appropriately to stress. The likelihood is that trained participants will hear what the other person is saying as "noise". This means that they will not get "hooked" and respond in a way that gives the other person even more ammunition to continue the argument or verbal attack.

Special Place develops a strong sense of self appreciation, self esteem and self confidence. The use of Special Place is such an integral part of the training, that this activity is often repeated at least twice during each session. Participants are asked to write down their images, and feelings about themselves while in their Special Place.

In the enhanced version of Special Place, participants are asked to touch part of their Special Place, silently say their name and a good quality that they have identified while in their Special Place. The exercise builds even more associations and good qualities and feelings in to it to

52

enable participants to have several ways of accessing their Special Place. With this access they can also access Intentional Behavior. Some people become so skilled with accessing their Special Place, that even the name "special place" will enable them to experience strong sensations of relaxation and various good qualities that they have. Due to the way this exercise is constructed, even people who claim they can't visualize are able to gain from the experience as other modalities besides vision are brought into the Special Place. For example, participants might be asked to hear whatever sounds they would hear in their Special Place. People who visualize themselves at the beach might hear the surf or the call of a seagull. People on a mountain top might hear the wind rustling the leaves on a tree. As has been mentioned, participants also touch part of their special place. One might feel the softness of beach sand or the strength or hardness of bolder on a mountain.

If participants wish to create their own recording of their Special Place, they may do so. However, most do not. Most people are able to create their own Special Place and don't need a recording due to the specific associations that they have of this imagery/experience.

The Special Place is designed to maximize one's sense of self (ME). It is one of the favorite techniques of most people. Because of the way this experience is designed, each person is able to create his own Special Place and does not need the use of a voice recording. Remember, Special Place is not meant to be an escapist technique. It is designed to be used in the midst of an interpersonal argument or even a verbal attack. Instead of getting distressed and resorted to an automatic behavior learned at an earlier time in one's live, a trained participant will often smile, realize what the other person is trying to do and stay in Intentional Behavior.

In order to get into an argument with someone, the other person has to "play the game". The other person needs to respond. So, person "A" tries to get person "B" to be angry. But person "B" doesn't take the bait and doesn't get hooked. The result is person "A" gives up and will probably experience disappointment or frustration that they could get person "B" into an argument or upset them. This is one of the many practical applications of Special Place, which is the key to Intentional behavior.

The Special Place Narration

The narration is done slowly, with pauses between sentences to give participants time to develop the images. This is the "simple" version.

Picture a place where you feel calm and peaceful, perhaps on a mountaintop. Take a few moments to see the objects below you. Notice how the trees just exist and the rocks exist and you feel peaceful and calm. In this Special Place you feel calm, relaxed and peaceful. Notice how the rocks are solid and strong and the trees are firmly rooted. Yet their leaves flow with the breeze. Notice whatever sounds you hear. Perhaps the rustling of leaves flowing with the wind. Maybe birds singing. And notice how you feel calm, relaxed and peaceful. Enjoy the calmness, peacefulness and relaxation that you feel in this Special Place and return back to wherever you are, keeping all those pleasant feelings and sensations. They are yours to experience whenever you want.

Summary

Celebrate ME is an essential part of the D.C.P. The key to accessing Intentional Behavior is to be in one's "ME". There are numerous ways to accomplish a strong sense of self. This chapter presented several different techniques for doing that ranging from some very simple techniques to more challenging ones.

It is also essential that participants understand the difference between bragging vs. self-appreciation. Most of us have not escaped "put downs", being called names and ridiculed when we were young children. Some of us as adult have continued to experience such distressing behavior by our peers, co-workers and acquaintances. Today such behavior is called "bullying". Celebrate ME offers a way of dealing with such behavior, strengthening one's sense of self esteem and recognizing one's good qualities.

A strong ME is necessary to access Intentional behavior and provides a way of dealing with the continuous bombardment of stress that we experience in the 21st century. There is one person that you can always depend upon and that person is – YOU! Living in a sea of change where technology constantly changes and brings about many changes in our society, it is essential to have a solid sense of self. Celebrate ME enables people to identify their positive qualities and understand no matter how badly you might feel, you still have those positive qualities no matter what is said or done to you.

An online version of Celebrate ME is available on the Web.

For more information go to www.designedchange.org. or simply Google "Designed Change."

Here are some excerpts of the Celebrate ME workshop.

NEW and GOOD Technique

This is a very simple technique to do, but rather complicated to explain how it works. I'm going to focus on how to do it. You simply identify something that made you feel good. It can be anything, anything at all as long as it is new and good. It might be some little thing, like trying a new breakfast cereal, or getting a letter from an old friend. It could be something like winning the lottery or getting a promotion at work. It doesn't matter what it is, as long as it is new and good.

Why do this technique? It's a stress reducer. It actually forces your brain to focus on something else other than distress (any uncomfortable feeling). This technique is portable, meaning that you can do it anywhere and I do mean anywhere. It's a great way to begin a meeting or a meal.

What is your New and Good?

_____

Old and Good – If you can't identify any New and Good things that have happened, how about some Old and Good experiences.

What is your Old and Good?

_____

Finally, if you can't identify any New and Goods or Old and Goods, ask yourself and answer this question – "What is the least bad thing that has happened to you lately?" This will usually produce a chuckle and then you will be able to identify either a New and Good or an Old and Good.

Another Celebration Technique – Self Appreciation

Identify a positive quality you have – something you appreciate about your self. Identify all the times you used this quality. Think of the specific <u>times</u> you used it. Next, identify, the various <u>places</u> you have used this quality. Finally, identify the <u>ways</u> that you have used this quality.

Times I've used this quality:

_____

Places I've used this quality:

_____

Ways I've used this quality:

_____

(Note: There may be some redundancy between the times, places and ways your have used this activity. The idea is to identify that you have used this quality many times).

The Inventory

Make a list of all your positive qualities and keep a running inventory. Keep adding positive qualities to your list. This is an on-going assignment. Use a notebook or create a file in your computer.

Chapter 4 – Feelings

The training in feelings is a delightful and practical explanation of what a feeling is, the various levels of feelings and how to change them. Although this information was developed many years ago, there still exists quite a lack of understanding about what feelings really are.

Much has been written about the Mind-Body Connection. The D.C.P. explains that feelings are physiological events that take place in our bodies and offers several techniques for either lowering the intensity of a feeling or actually changing it.

Society still promotes many myths about feelings, such as: they are ethereal and certain types of feelings are okay for one gender, but not for the other. For example, what do you call an angry man? (Most would say either "an angry man" or "sir". But, what do you call an angry woman? (a bitch). Conversely, it is okay for a woman to act frightened. But what is a frightened man called? (a coward, sissy, yellow belly, wimp, etc). It is amazing that such beliefs and behaviors still are perpetuated as the D.C.P. addressed these issues over 20 years ago.

What is a Feeling?

A feeling is a physiological event that takes place in your body. Originally, feelings were used for survival purposes – to prepare the body. I will talk more about this later.

The D.C.P explains feelings using a seven step sequence.

1. **Event**. There is an event – something happens.

2. **Perception**. The event is perceived. What actually happened and what one perceives may not necessarily be the same.

3. **Chemical Injection** – The brain releases various chemicals that flow into the blood stream. One chemical that is often released is adrenalin, which stimulates the nervous system.

4. **Physiological Change** – the chemical injection results in a physiological change

5. **Monitor** – We have monitors all over are bodies. These are nerve endings, which help us to become aware of changes.

6. **Feeling** – we become aware of a feeling.

7. **Contract with Behavior**. We have an agreement with ourselves. When we feel a certain feeling, we act a certain way. This can get us into trouble. If one feels angry and acts aggressively it can result in problems. However, you do not need to act upon the feeling and the D.C.P. teaches how to interrupt this and the entire cycle. This last step creates a new event and the entire sequence begins all over. Thus one can get angry about the fact that one is angry or anxious about the fact that one is anxious, etc. What results in effect is a feedback cycle with steps six and seven returning back to step one. The feeling creates a new event as does the behavior.

Further explanation

Without going into a philosophical discussion, what we perceive as an "event" isn't necessarily what actually happens. Recall that distress distorts perception. However, regardless of what one perceives, if you view something as stressful or as threatening, then it is to you and the entire sequence of a feeling will run. The fact that distress distorts perception, a well documented fact, greatly increases the likelihood that what we perceive as a threat may not really be a threat. But it doesn't matter. Once we perceive something as a threat, our bodies respond and we react.

Consider this scenario. You are walking in an unfamiliar area of a city. You see a stranger walking towards you and he is carrying a big stick. The street is deserted except for you and this man coming towards you with a big stick. Most people would perceive this as a threat or a potential threat. As he gets closer, you realize that the man is walking with a limp and is using the stick to help him walk. You feel a bit relieved, but still are "on guard" in a heightened sense of alert. As a precaution, you cross the street and are relieved to see that the man with the big stick continues on his way

Chemical Injection

We now know that there are many chemicals that can be released into the blood stream by the brain. Common ones are adrenalin, noradrenalin, and dopamine, just to name a few. These chemicals are very powerful and often serve to energize the body triggering what is known as the "fight or flight" syndrome. Your body becomes energized to fight (deal with the threat) or run away.

Physiological Change

In essence, a feeling is a physiological change that takes place in your body. While feelings remain somewhat of a mystery to many people, there is some common knowledge about feelings that indicate their *physical* nature. Such expressions as "hot with angry" or "cold with fear" really do describe some of the physiological changes that feelings bring when we experience them. There are several monitoring devices that can record some of these changes. Bio Feedback equipment has been around for years. One such device is a galvanic skin response meter that can detect changes in the skin. Lie detector machines also know as polygraphs can also detect changes in feeling. An EKG or cardiogram machine, used by doctors to detect changes in the heart is another device that can be used to detect feelings. Stress, more accurately, distress, will raise heart rate and blood pressure readings.

However, you don't need to go out purchase any of these expensive devices to monitor your feelings. All you need to do is pay attention to your body and you can detect all sorts of things. For example, right now, feel the chair that you are sitting upon. Now feel the clothing on your body. Now pay attention to the temperature in the room. Is it too warm, too cold, or just right? We actually monitor all these things and many more, all at the same time. But, we are not usually aware of any one thing unless we focus upon it.

Back in the 1970's "mood rings" were popular. These were rings that turned colors depending upon your mood. In reality, it was nothing more than a heat sensor that changed with the blood flow in your finger. Thus, if you were relaxed it would turn blue, indicating a good mood. However, if you became anxious or frightened, it would change colors as the blood would shift from your fingers to protect the vital organs. The rings really weren't an accurate indicator of mood, but were fun to wear and popular for a time.

Feeling— As stated earlier, a feeling is a physiological event that occurs in your body. The D.C.P. teaches how to manage feelings by strengthening those feelings that you want and weakening those that you don't want. There are specific techniques for doing this that will be discussed in the Feelings Workshop. A major component of the DCP is learning about feelings: what they are, what they do and most important, how to change them. Despite popular myths about feelings they can be changed and one can also learn how to separate the feeling from the behavior

Contract with Behavior – this is an agreement that you have with yourself. With each particular feeling there is a particular behavior or behaviors. Most people don't know how to distinguish the difference and aren't even aware that there is a difference. So when they feel angry, they act angry. When they feel anxious, they act anxious. When they feel depressed, they act depressed, etc. Here is a description of the common behaviors for some common feelings.

FEELING	BEHAVIOR
Anger	Aggressive, hostile, raising one's voice, making a fist to more violent behaviors
Anxious	Acting restless, pacing, nervousness, restlessness
Sad/Depressed	Withdrawal, quiet, negative thinking and negative talk
Fear	Withdrawal, shaking, trembling

There are many other feelings both pleasant and unpleasant. The point to understand is that the feeling and the behavior are NOT the same and they can be separated. If they are not separated, the feeling can intensify. This applies to both pleasant and unpleasant feelings. To intensify any feelings, simply focus on them. Think about it. Recall times that you have experienced that feeling - when and where.

At nearly every step of this sequence, feelings can be managed. While it may not be possible to eliminate an event, how you perceive that event matters a great deal. Recall that distress distorts perception. Be aware that your perception of the event may be distorted.

Chemical Injection – this is by far one of the most popular ways of dealing with feelings by using alcohol or drugs (legal or illegal). However, if you learn to change and/or manage your feelings you will not need to resort to using alcohol or drugs to change your feelings.

Physiological Change – We can bring about physical changes in our bodies using a variety of methods, including exercise, relaxation and even laughter.

Monitors – As has already been discussed, we have built in monitors throughout our bodies. By developing some awareness we can tune into these monitors. For example, feel the clothing on your body. Now feel the chair you are sitting in. Now feel the temperature of the room. We are doing these things all the time, but usually we are unaware of them.

Feeling – We can change any feeling using a variety of methods. One way to do that is to focus on a desired feeling such as relaxation. Think of all the times, ways and places that you have felt relaxed. The D.C.P. offers numerous ways of changing feelings. This example is only one of many.

Contract with Behavior – it is vital to understand the difference between the actual feeling and the behavior that usually accompanies it. A behavior pattern can be interrupted and changed through practice. It might sound like a lot of work, but actually, it can be a lot of fun. The D.C.P. offers specific techniques for interrupting and changing behavior.

Levels of Feelings

There are three levels of feelings: primary, associative and interpersonal. These levels of feelings are best described by a story that has been repeatedly told (by Tom Sargent at various training sessions and workshops).

Imagine you walk into a room and there is a real live lion in the room. You run out of the room terrified. This is an example of a primary feeling. The "fight or flight" (stress response) syndrome kicks in and you ran out of the room. We inherited this from our great ancestor – the cave man. When the cave man ventured out of his cave and came face to face with saber tooth tiger, he got a shot of adrenalin and either stood there and fought the beast or ran like hell. This is an example of the primary level of feelings

Now, each time you walk past that room you feel frightened because you associate the lion being in that room (even if the lion is no longer there). This is an example of the associative level of feelings.

Finally, a friend comes up to you, comforts you by embracing you and giving you hug and acknowledging how terrified you must have been when you saw that lion. Now you are feeling close and warm instead of terrified. Now, whenever you want to feel close and warm you feel terrified. This is an interpersonal use of a feeling. You might think that is this crazy or not rational? It's quite common and it merely demonstrates the interpersonal use of a feeling.

Types of Feelings

Ask someone how they feel and they'll often say, I feel "good". But if you ask them to define "good", they may have a difficult time. On the other hand, if someone says they don't feel so good, they can list several different types of feelings that describe how they feel. When it comes to describing "good" feelings, many people are at a loss. Most people either describe feelings as "good" or "bad". During the Feelings Workshop, participants are often asked to brainstorm different types of "good" feelings. By "good" feelings, I mean feelings that feel "good" to have as opposed to distress feelings that always feel uncomfortable.

Some people like to classify feelings as positive or negative. While some feelings definite feel more pleasant than others, the D.C.P. recognizes a feeling simply as a physiological event. Most of the distress feelings we experience originate from primary feelings we have that helped to keep our ancestor, the cave man, alive. Fear, in particular is a specific response to the fight or flight syndrome and it can also serve as a great motivator. But too much fear can be debilitating.

Fight or Flight Syndrome Lives On

It's interesting that what was designed to help us survive, the "fight or flight" syndrome, can actually cause harm to us today. To be sure, if you're in a dangerous situation, this syndrome automatically occurs. But the problem with living in the 21 century is oftentimes we perceive that we are in danger, but the danger isn't real or not as much of a threat as we perceive it to be. Yet, the fight or flight syndrome continues to occur.

For example, you're about to cross the street and suddenly a Mac truck comes speeding down the street. You instantly react and jump out of the way. This is the result of the fight or flight syndrome. Now imagine you're driving and suddenly you see the flashing lights behind you and realize you are being pulled over by a police officer. You get that sinking feeling in your stomach and you feel scared. Once again the fight or flight syndrome is at work. Of course fighting or fleeing from a police officer will only get you into more trouble.

Sometimes we get into a situation where we repeatedly keep getting stimulated in such a way that the fight or flight syndrome occurs again and again and again. Students have often reported a situation where they dread going to a particular class because the instructor may call on them when they are not prepared. This type of repeated long term stress is actually much worse on your body than one intense incident. Remember, however that stress is largely a perception of a threat. If you view something as stressful, then it is. The perception of stress is highly individualized. This explains why someone may experience joy when riding on a roller coaster and another person might find the experience to quite distressing.

Techniques

Several of the techniques used to manage feelings have been discussed in the previous chapter. While you may recognize several of them, you will also see how they are used specifically to change and manage feelings. Prior to D.C.P. training, most people don't believe that it is possible to change a feeling. Most people don't understand what a feeling is, let alone know how to change it. Yet, any feeling can be changed and here is a variety of techniques to do that.

New and Goods – As discussed previously, this is a simple and quick way to change your feelings, by focusing on something that is pleasant, as opposed to thinking about something that is unpleasant (distressing).

Old and Good – a variation to be used if you can not recall anything that is "new and good". In that case, identify something this is old and good.

Least Bad Thing – If you can not even recall something that was old and good, then answer this question. "What is the least bad thing that has happened to you lately"?

Scanning - Using this technique you focus briefly on a specific feeling and identity a time or place that you have experienced it. Some pleasant feelings you might like to scan include: joy, peacefulness, confidence, energetic, calm/relaxed. There are actually many other pleasant feelings. Here are some other feelings you might wish to scan:

Happy, powerful, intelligent, centered, appreciated, loved, strong, respected, desired.

"I like how I feel _____ when I _____." - This is a simple technique that allows you to identify the feeling associated with a particular activity. Sometimes it is easier to reverse the sentence to "When I _____ I feel _____.

Here are some examples: I like how I feel <u>strong</u> when I lift <u>weights</u>.

Here is another example: I like how I feel <u>creative</u> when I <u>compose music</u>.

The following is the reversed sentence: When I <u>lift weights</u> I feel <u>strong</u>.

Because many people are illiterate when it comes to identifying feelings, some people find it easier to begin with the activity and then identify the feeling. While the technique is amazingly simple, it is also amazingly effective. What this technique does is have you focus on something you like to do and identify the feeling associated with it. In a way, it is a double attack against distress because you focus on something you enjoy doing, which can reduce distress in itself. In addition, you identify the pleasant feeling associated with the activity.

Variation on Enjoyable Activities – If you do the Enjoyable Activities technique discussed in the previous chapter, you could go back and identify a pleasant feeling for each activity. You could also use the list of enjoyable activities to do this technique.

Remember, that focusing upon any feeling intensifies it. If you focus on anxiety you get more of it. If you focus on pleasure you get more of that.

Random Pleasant Memories – This technique works best when someone either reads or calls out a list of random pleasant memories. As a variation, you could record your own list, but many people get distracted or even distressed listening to their own voice. You could also make a list of some memories. However, the original format seems to work best.

Here is an example of the actual technique: think about a parade, a puppy, a nice sunny day, the beach, a delicious meal, getting a pleasant but unexpected email, a crackling fire, listening to enjoyable music, lunch with a friend, doing what you like to do.

The idea is to move fairly rapidly from one memory to another. Random Pleasant Memories have been known to eliminate headaches and also help people relax and fall asleep. The technique is quite simple and quite effective. It works by having you focus on something that is pleasant as opposed to something that is distressing.

Recalling a Memory with Details - Using this technique you focus on one specific memory and recall as much detail as possible. Here's an example – recall a vacation you took and really enjoyed. Where were you? What did you do? What was the weather like? Were you indoors or outdoors? What were you wearing? What sounds did you hear?

Most people can do this without any assistance. Just ask someone to pick a specific memory that is a really good one. It is often amazing how the details come back. It's like running a movie. Many people can actually re-experience the feelings that they had. Given a choice of being distressed or recalling a pleasant memory and re-experiencing those pleasant feelings, it makes little sense to choose to remain distressed.

Special Place – This is a guided imagery/visualization with built in associations. The Special Place is an important technique because it promotes a strong sense of self (ME) which is a central part of the D.C.P. This technique brings with it a number of pleasant feelings. It is a powerful technique that includes a positive sense of self, feelings of relaxation and a keen awareness of one's good qualities. The technique is not designed to be used to escape. Rather it is designed to be used right in the midst of distressing situation. Individuals immediately experience the positive effects of this technique. However, with practice you can learn to use it in a distressing situation and be fully aware of where you are and what you are doing and how you are interacting with whoever is causing you to feel distressed.

Celebrating Good Qualities – this is a central part of Celebrating ME and is a particularly good technique to do to combat ridicule, put downs and other invalidating statements. If you're being verbally attacked, instead of getting angry and upset, identify some of your good qualities to yourself. If you have a really strong ME, a strong sense of self, you will hear such invalidating statements simply as noise. You will know that there is no truth to what someone is saying and you might even laugh. Imagine if someone came up to a famous singer, such as Andrea Bocelli and said, "Mr. Bocelli, you are a lousy singer. You can't even carry a tune." That is such a ridiculous statement that probably Andrea would just laugh and walk away. I doubt if he'd start feeling insecure or "bad" about himself. By celebrating your good qualities you can continue to maintain pleasant feelings about yourself even if someone says some uncomplimentary remark to you.

Down Feelings – By celebrating down feelings, feelings that don't feel good to you, you can actually lessen the intensity of such feelings. As has been previously discussed, celebrating means appreciating. By genuinely appreciating how good you are at having and maintaining a "down" feeling, you can actually lessen its intensity. For example, you might say something like – "I'm really good at feeling guilty. Get me to feel guilty and you own me. I'll do anything. I'm so good at feeling guilty that I could teach you and others how to feel guilty". Now, if this sounds rather silly or even ridiculous, on one hand it is. But on the other hand it is the silliness or ridiculousness that weakens the distress feeling.

Mocking Patterns – Behavior patterns like to be taken seriously. When you start making fun or mocking a behavior pattern, you will weaken it. The way you mock a pattern is similar to celebrating down feelings or mocking them. Patterns often have intense distress feelings attached to them. Therefore, it is important to find ways of lessening their intensity.

Pattern Interruption - A pattern is like a chain link fence. You can't break the link. But you can change the link by adding to it. All you need to do is do one thing differently. For example, if you're running a depressed pattern, stop and smile. Put a nice big smile on your face and say, "I feel so wonderful! Be careful! You can really interrupt a good depression by doing this. Remember, part of every distress pattern contains distressing feelings. By changing the pattern you in effect change the feelings. However, changing a pattern requires first being aware it,

70

interrupting it and replacing it with some new behavior. Then you need to practice the new behavior.

With any pattern, if you do something different you in effect change the pattern

There is another technique that will be discussed in the chapter on Co-Counseling called, the "Interrupter" which can be used to interrupt behavior patterns.

The Inventory – This is newer technique that I created. It consists of keeping a journal of all your positive qualities. It's an on-going technique that you can continue to do throughout your life. Whenever you want, you can go through your Inventory and look at all the positive qualities you have. The technique can be done when you're distressed or not distressed. Keep adding to your inventory. It is a life long process.

Summary:

Feelings are physical and can be changed. They are physiological events in our bodies. Feelings can be explained in a seven step sequence. There is a contract with behavior. When you feel a certain way, you act a certain way. However, this can be separated. Finally, there are three different levels of feelings: primary, associative and interpersonal. Each step of the sequence of a feeling can be interrupted.

There continues to exist much confusion and misinformation about feelings. Many people do not consider feelings to be physical. Some people still think that feelings are ethereal and are like clouds that can fall upon you. Many people think that you must be strong and not show your feelings. In certain situations this is appropriate. Many professionals are trained to be this way, such as people who give the news.

Society still designates that certain feelings are acceptable for women, but not for men. A frightened woman is called a frightened woman. But a frightened man is called a sissy, wimp, yellow belly, etc. Conversely, an angry man is called an angry man, or "sir". But an angry woman is often called a bitch.

There are different levels of feelings: primary, associative and interpersonal. Primary feelings were originally used for survival. Much has been said about the "flight or fight syndrome, which often involves fear. The body prepares itself to do battle or run.

The Associative level of feeling is simply an association with that feeling and something else. People associate feelings with all sorts of things: music, restaurants, clothing, buildings, people, etc.

The Interpersonal level or use of a feeling is when the feeling is used for another purpose. For example, if a child gets scared and gets a hug every time he feels scared, now all he has to do to feel closeness is get scared and he'll get a hug. It is not just children who do things like this. Adults do as well.

Any feeling will intensify if you focus upon it – both pleasant and distressing feelings. Many people continue to focus on distressing situations and feelings, thereby intensifying the distressing feeling. For example, John, a customer service representative had a difficult caller. The caller swore at him and hung up. John kept thinking about that call as he answered other callers all day long. He felt distressed and wasn't as sharp as he usually is. Consequently, his day didn't go very well and he seemed to be attracting difficult callers all day. Actually, because John was distressed, he was noticing distress much more intensely. That actually interfered with his ability to respond to the calls.

When John came home, he continued to think about his "bad day". The entire day became "bad" because of one caller. The more John focused on that difficult caller, the more distressed he became. However, John could turn this whole experience around by focusing on something that is non-distressing. What about all the extremely happy and grateful callers he has had? Remember, when we are distressed, we don't have access to Intentional behavior and certain information. John could use any number of techniques to manage his distress or he can continue to dwell upon it and make it worse. Most of us continue to dwell upon it and make it worse, until we learn that we don't need to do that. Any of the techniques discussed in this chapter can help us change or manage distressing feelings. Whatever you focus on intensifies – pleasant or distressing.

A strong sense of self (ME) plays an important role in the management of feelings and is a central component to the D.C.P. Often times when we feel "bad" about ourselves, we can change the way we feel by doing the Special Place technique.

There are many techniques for changing a feeling. Feelings influence our behavior and our inter-personal relations that will be discussed in the next chapter.

Here are some exercises for changing feelings.

Scanning: (for about 1 minute each)

1. times you have felt relaxed
2. times you have felt angry
3. times you have felt peaceful

New and Goods – Identify some New and Good experiences, (aka Recent Pleasant Experiences):

I like how I feel _____ **when I** _____ . Fill in the blanks. Do this exercise several times and each time identify the feelings and the activity.

Celebrate ME – There are many ways to celebrate your "ME". Make a list of positive qualities that you have. To enhance each quality, scan the times, places or ways that you've experienced that quality.

Chapter 5 - Interpersonal Relations Workshop

Much has already been discussed about the interpersonal use of feelings in the chapter on Feelings. It bears mentioning again that sometimes we use feelings for inter-personal reasons, such as: we use fear to get love and attention as was described in the story about the lion.

Here's a little story that will introduce you to Inter-personal Relations. One day, I meet Meg, a friend of mine who invites me over to her place for a cup of coffee. Meg makes me a cup of coffee and pours herself a cup of tea. Now, I don't really care that much for coffee, but I don't want to say anything to Meg because she graciously invited me over for coffee.

About a week later, Meg and I meet at her house for a meeting and John joins us. Meg proceeds to make me a cup of coffee and pours John and herself a cup of tea. Something even stranger happens. I actually begin to enjoy coffee but only at Meg's place. Sound strange? Welcome to the wild world of interpersonal relations!

The D.C.P. offers several skills to foster and improve inter-personal relations. These skills include:

- Communication – including listening and the use of "I" statements

- Validation of Self

- Validation of the Relationship aka the "Homework"

- The Language of the Relationship – what the behavior is saying

- Use of Stress Management techniques (Feeling's Management)

A central part of Inter-Personal Relations and all of the D.C.P. material is the concept of "ME". How we relate to other people is reflected by how we relate to ourselves. By focusing on your good qualities, the things you like about yourself, you actually strengthen your sense of self esteem.

Another major theme of this workshop is communication skills, including listening and "active listening", sometimes called reflective listening or paraphrasing. Listening is difficult because you can think faster than I can talk. Most people can easily get distracted and stop paying attention to what is being said. To help people focus, the D.C.P. teaches people to use "active listening", sometimes called "Reflective Listening". However the version that the D.C.P. uses is a little different.

Most Reflective Listening courses have you repeat back what you heard being said, but include a phrase "what I heard you say is ...". The D.C.P. doesn't allow this phrase for several reasons. It can be used as an excuse. Your paraphrasing may not be accurate, but by using this phrase you can always put the blame on the speaker. *What I heard you say was .... That may not be what you meant, but that's what I heard.* Furthermore, the use of this phrase, "what I heard you say was ..." can serve to put distance between the two people. It can become a type of game that an insecure person might play. Instead of admitting that one didn't understand what you said, one can use that phrase.

The D.C.P. recommends avoiding this phrase and providing either an actual paraphrase or a summary. The speaker can then clarify what he/she meant. This has proven to be much more effective than using the phrase, "What I hear you saying is …". If you are the listener, don't worry about "getting it right". The speaker will let you know if you are correct or not and will clarify. However, when you use that phrase, "What I hear you saying is …", you are setting yourself up as a person who never misunderstands. This can actually lead to an argument between the speaker and the listen. It can also generate distress for the speaker, who might think, "No one understands me". Other distress recordings may come into play. Therefore, it is much more effective to paraphrase what you heard said or if several sentences were spoken, provide a summary. If you, as the listener, didn't get it right, the speaker will let you know. If you're the speaker and you were misunderstood, you can provide further clarification.

Along with Active Listening, the issue of stress is addressed. Whenever a speaker mentions a topic that is stressful to the listener, listening becomes very difficult. Therefore, stress reduction is emphasized.

Many years ago I witnessed a very amusing demonstration of how stress can interfere with listening. Tom Sargent was doing an exercise with a participant and Tom told the participant that at some point he would say something that would cause the participant to feel distressed. All the participant had to do was repeat back what he heard. All was fine until Tom said to the participant, "why do you have a beard"? Immediately, the participant became angry and responded, "what do you mean why do I have a beard? At that point everyone, including the participant burst out laughing. (Note: Tom had a beard as well).

Another piece of this workshop focuses on what become known as *The Homework*. This was an exercise for couples consisting of three parts: 1) validation of self, 2) validation of one's partner and 3) validation of the relationship. Then the other partner also had a turn to do the same thing. This "exercise" was very useful in helping couples who were having difficulty in their relationship. By validating oneself, one's partner and the relationship, new and greater appreciations were discovered which served to enhance the relationship.

Other topics in this workshop included decision making, with an emphasis on consensus and conflict resolution where a synergistic result could take place where the results could be greater than the conflict itself, by using the D.C.P. With consensus, both sides win. But with compromise, each side gives up something. While most conflict resolution often focuses on compromise, the D.C.P. emphasized synergy. The idea is for each side to state what they want, then work together to make it happen. With compromise, each person gives up something. With synergy, people often get more than what they thought was possible. It is not always possible for synergy to take place. However, amazing results can take place once adversaries begin working together to make that happen. Stress reduction and validation of one's adversary are necessary for this to happen. Even changing positions of where one is sitting at a table can make a difference. The D.C.P. provides many additional techniques for resolving conflicts and this piece of training is an entire program in itself.

Decision-making is an entire topic in itself and is not exclusively a part of the D.C.P.. The focus within D.C.P. training is on consensus. Individuals who make decisions often do so on an emotional level. Often a person will make a decision, then look for evidence to support the decision. This is actually backwards. A decision needs to be made by examining the facts. Feelings, however, do affect decision-making. The time to make a decision is when you are <u>not</u> in a lot of stress, because "distress impairs thinking". Unfortunately, oftentimes decisions are made when one is under a lot of stress. Decision-making is a complex cognitive skill that is impeded by feelings. While many people pride themselves of being logical in their decision-making, oftentimes, their decisions are greatly influenced by various feelings.

Conflict Resolution is not exclusively part of the DCP. The use of "I" statements, assertiveness training and decision making are not exclusively part of the DCP, either, but like conflict resolution, are significantly enhanced by the D.C.P. by combining these skills with knowledge of distress, feelings and behavior.

The following is a brief summary of how conflict resolution is used within the D.C.P.. First each person has a turn to express what they want using "I" statements. To make certain their needs or wants are heard, the opposition uses reflective listening and repeats back via paraphrasing what was said. In this manner errors both from the speaker and listener can be corrected.

After each party states their position, they literally change seating positions at the table. This sometimes helps to gain a better viewpoint of what the other party wants. Then they enter a type of problem solving where they try and work together so each party gets what they want. Oftentimes synergy results, where the end result is greater than what initially was expected. This is not always the case. To facilitate this, each party is asked to validate the other party and to use stress reduction techniques to deal with any stress. In order for this to happen, both parties need to be trained in the D.C.P.. It should be mentioned that the person who facilitates this resolution must also be highly trained and skilled.

The D.C.P. recognizes five controlling factors that affect interpersonal relations. These five factors include:

1. highly charged conditioned interpersonal responses,

2. the interpersonal meaning of behavior,

3. interpersonal contracts and group behavior,

4. the internal conflicts between the need for autonomy and the need for community,

5. the action-reaction process for group change.

(Sargent 1984)

Conditioned interpersonal responses are behavior patterns. Sargent describes them as "recordings of earlier experiences in relationships" (1984). These recordings or behavior patterns are triggered by distress. They are repetitive, old familiar responses that are often inappropriate (Sargent 1984). "The earliest of these conditioned interpersonal responses are learned in early childhood" (Sargent pp 52, 1984).

Interpersonal Meaning of Behavior

The interpersonal meaning of behavior refers to how we act when relating to others, whether a personal or non-personal relationship. Since most of human behavior is learned, we use behaviors that we learned from an earlier time in our lives – usually from childhood. Most of us grew up relating to others in a unique way – we were little and everyone else was big. The parent/child relationship way of relating is still dominant in most relationships today. Teacher/student, boss/worker, doctor/patient are all examples of this way of relating. The D.C.P. offers an alternative to this by relating to people from your "ME". However, without training, most of the time we revert back to earlier methods of relating using old patterns of behavior that are triggered by distress. These are automatic patterns that are rigid and repetitive providing little if any access to Intentional behavior. A key to recognizing such behavior is to pay attention to your feelings, especially uncomfortable feelings which trigger the automatic response. If you keep getting into the same type of relationship or keep meeting people that displease you because of the way they act, it is quite possible that you are contributing to this type of relationship by bringing your own behavior into the relationship. What you are doing in the relationship refers to the interpersonal meaning of behavior.

"Most interpersonal relationships are managed through feelings designed to control the behavior of others" (Sargent pp 57, 1984). The feelings trigger the automatic response in us and when reinforced, are likely to strengthen. The plot thickens here, because often it is not just your patterns that are activated and running, but the other person in the relationship as well. Thus, oftentimes there are two interpersonal patterns of behavior running. In fact, it is quite common to see this happening when two individuals get together and trigger each other's patterns. It's like watching an old movie where you know what each person is going to say. Frequently, this is what happens when two people have an argument. It doesn't take long for reason and logic to go out the window and be replaced by two people's patterns battling each other. They way out of this is to have a strong "ME" and pay attention to your distress and manage those feelings. This is part of what the D.C.P. offers.

Interpersonal Contracts and Group Behavior

Just as person has a "contract with behavior", people also have interpersonal contracts with others. This involves certain ways of behaving that is unaware to the individuals involved. The problem of accessing Intentional behavior becomes even more compounded and difficult within a group. Each group has its own culture and ways of doing things. Certain behaviors are permitted while others are forbidden. Individuals will, without knowing it, conform to the exact requirements of the group or be excluded (Sargent 1984). The group climate, all the rules and regulations, all of the permitted behaviors are part of an individual's Automatic behavior mode. When the climate of the group is changed, the individual's behavior will change as well. Optimal group functioning requires excellent communication among its members, and individual differences. However, this requires a deliberate conscious effort and many groups are unaware at the time of what is happening. It is not uncommon for people to leave a group meeting wondering what just happened. "How did we get onto that topic?" or "what just happened?" are somewhat common questions people have when they realize something went awry.

Internal Conflicts and the Need for Autonomy and the Need for Community

All groups large and small struggle with the need for the individual and the need for the group. Differences occur even among the most cohesive groups. How these differences are handled becomes tantamount to the success of the group. If distress is allowed to run rampant, the outcome can be very predictable. However, when people respond from their "ME", a maximum amount of alternatives can be found.

Action-Reaction Process for Group Change

Although I never studied physics, there is a law of physics that basically says – for every action, there is reaction. The same thing applies to groups. Something happens and the group reacts and this becomes part of an on-going process. While the group has its own climate and culture, it consists of individual members. Groups change over time. Members come and go which change the dynamics of a group. Some groups eventually split and some fall apart. Groups that are based upon trust, where individuals feel "safe" and willing to express their ideas and opinions are much stronger than groups based upon fear. "Groups constantly disrupt and rebuild themselves" (Sargent pp60, 1984).

These five factors that have been discussed affect interpersonal relations. The role of learned behavior patterns and stress can not be underestimated. Each of us have are own behavior patterns of relating (usually based upon a parent/child relationship experience). What frequently results when two people have an argument is two behavior patterns battling against each other. This will be very apparent to an observer, but not to the two people arguing.

It is not by chance that people keep getting into the same type of relationship again and again, even though this is not what they desire. Do you think it's just 'bad luck' that the wife of an alcoholic will divorce her husband and marry another alcoholic?

The patterns of relating that we learned as children still affect us today. They are triggered by distress and we are often unaware of what is happening. A key to changing these automatic responses is to pay attention to feelings, especially noting any distress feelings. Remember, that nearly all of us grew up in a world where we were little and everyone else was big. Parent/child relationships still exist today in our adult world and are very prevalent.

The D.C.P. offers a variety of ways to unravel these complex behaviors and change them. The first step is to develop a strong sense of self ("ME"). With a strong sense of self, one can examine parts of one's behavior and gain access to Intentional behavior.

It is also necessary and essential to be able to manage feelings. When in an interpersonal or personal relationship, distress often occurs. Recognizing distress is the key to changing one's behavior. It is the distress that triggers the automatic response. Therefore it becomes imperative to recognize distress, be aware of it and reduce its intensity.

The role of communication also plays a key role in interpersonal relations. Most problems in relationships can be traced to poor or miscommunication where one person interprets what was said differently than what the speaker meant. These misunderstandings can greatly expand and generate a lot of distress. The person you talk with may misunderstand what you meant and become angry. Next, they begin acting cold or even hostile towards you. You in term become annoyed, hurt or angry. In a matter of minutes both people are running automatic behavior patterns which only compound and add to the confusion and distress. The cycle repeats and escalates until the conversation is completely broken off and even violent behavior can result. It can be a messy job to fix this situation and many of the distressed feelings need to be managed or discharged.

One of the ways the D.C.P handles a situation like this is to teach people good communication skills, especially the use of "I" statements. As has already been discussed, an "I" statement begins with the word "I", followed by what you want.

Instead of saying, "You be quiet, it's my turn to talk", a more effective statement might be "I want to say something and I want you to understand what I am saying".

To assure that the other person does comprehend, "reflective listening" can be used. This is where the listening reflects back what was said, in their own words and without the phrase "what I hear you saying is ...". This method of communication, "I" statements and reflective listening is especially helpful for resolving conflicts.

However, oftentimes the feelings that people have are so intense, that they first need to either discharge them or manage them. Both of these methods have been discussed in previous chapters. It may not be feasible, (although highly desirable and effective) for two parties to "manage" or "discharge" their feelings. If they are able to use "I" statements and reflective listening, often a conflict can be resolved and at the very least, both parties will have a much clearer understanding of what is desired.

Oftentimes the most mundane topic can lead to an argument. Consider the following, where the husband forgets to put the cap back on the toothpaste.

Wife: how many times have I told you to please put the cap back on the toothpaste tube?

Husband: Listen, I have more important things to think about than putting the cap back on the toothpaste tube. I have a very responsible job.

Wife; What the heck do think I do all day? I don't just sit around playing Solitaire.

Husband: I didn't say you did.

Wife: Well you implied that I did

Husband: No I didn't

Wife: Yes you did. You never listen to me (introducing a new topic for battle).

Husband: That's not true, I do listen to you.

Wife; No you don't. Are you calling me a liar?

Husband: I never said that.

Wife: You don't have to say it

Husband: If I say something it's no good, if I don't say something it also is no good. I can't say anything to you without an argument happening.

Wife: well none of this would happen if you'd put the darn cap back on the toothpaste. (returning back to the main argument)

Husband: "I've heard enough of this, I'm going out for a walk.

Wife: yeah, you always get to leave and I'm stuck cleaning up your mess. (introducing a broader issue) Well I'm sick of it.

Husband: (as he's walking out the door), I'd hardly call putting cap on a tube of toothpaste cleaning up a mess.

Wife: (repeats what he said in a mimicking voice)

Husband; Don't mimic me

Wife: (Mimics him even more and adds) maybe I should become a slob like you are

Husband: (now standing outside in the walkway), I am NOT a slob

Wife: Yes you are! (slams the door and locks it).

You can see how quickly things can escalate. New topics are introduced and the focus of the argument ends focusing whether or not the husband is a slob. Tempers flare and distress intensifies with each additional comment. At this point neither party can sit down and calmly discuss and identify what is upsetting them. The distress must be diffused. However, sometimes it isn't and explosions keep occurring eventually reaching the point where neither party can talk to the other without another argument ensuing.

Now, multiply this situation by 5 or ten people and imagine two groups of people each equally convinced that they are right and are unwilling to talk to the opposing party, because, they won't listen. It is essential to lower the stress level of each person.

Using the D.C.P. a conflict resolution model might begin by asking each person to share a New and Good, after providing a brief explanation for the request. Next, it might be necessary to explain the effects of distress – how perceptions can become distorted, thinking is impaired and automatic behaviors become triggered.

The role of "ME" in all of this is essential. People need to appreciate themselves. Then next step would be for them to appreciate each other, especially in the example of the husband and wife. The "Homework" would be a good exercise for both to do (discussed earlier).

When people have lowered their stress level to a sufficient point where they can actually speak to each other, the use of "I" statements and reflective listening would prove very helpful

After both parties have a clear understanding of what each person wants or needs, both can work towards resolution. Oftentimes, when people use this process they become aware of how their spouse feels and remark, "I never knew you felt that way".

When both parties understand each other's needs, oftentimes they can work together to solve each other's problems. When this happens synergy results where the results can be greater than the original problem. Oftentimes a list of possible solutions can be generated with both parties contributing towards the solution. This is only possible after the distress has been managed.

This entire process does not take place instantly. It may require several meetings. There is a lot of information that each party must understand and a lot of the material is experiential. This is perhaps a unique difference between the D.C.P. and other disciplines or approaches. While the D.C.P. is theoretical, it is also experiential and many of the skills and techniques can be applied, instantly. It's one thing to talk about reducing stress. It's another matter to have someone actually reduce their stress by sharing some New and Goods.

In summary, the Inter-Personal Relations Workshop included a combination of material from the Feelings Workshop and Celebrate ME workshop in addition to Communication Skills, Decision Making, Conflict Resolution and "The Homework".

Here is sequence of the various skills that would be presented for the Interpersonal Skills Workshop:

1. The Need for a Strong Sense of Self ("ME"). Several techniques for Celebrating ME would be presented/reviewed

2. The role of feelings – what they are and how they affect behavior. Ways of managing feelings would be presented. Some discharge techniques might be introduced.

3. The role of behavior patterns and their effect upon interpersonal and personal relations

4. Communication Skills –

    a) Use of "I" Statements

    b) Reflective Listening

5. Levels of Feelings and Interpersonal Meaning of Feeling

6. The "Homework"

The order might change somewhat depending upon the group of people. An emphasis is always placed on "hands-on" training as opposed to theory. A great deal of learning is experiential. Various techniques are used to lower the stress level of the group resulting in more trust and people feeling safe enough to share information.

A typical training program consists of some brief presentations, following by various exercises and activities to actually learn and practice the skills and techniques presented. Opportunities are provided for discussion and sharing.

The D.C.P. provides an alternative to relating to each other in the role of parent/child. What the Process offers is relating to each other self to self. All too often we relate to each other by roles and most of these ways of relating are really parent/child relationships. With the amount of patterned behavior that each of us has, it is no wonder that relationships are fraught with misunderstandings which usually lead to more problems. Remember, once people get distressed, they revert to patterned behavior, which is rigid, repetitive and renders access to Intentional behavior nearly impossible.

Agreement Strategies

The Agreement Strategies were created by Sargent in the later development of the D.C.P.

"The purpose of the Agreement Strategies is to extend agreement and at the same time advocate creative conflict" (Sargent pp1 1988).

Sargent created three main Agreement Strategies:

1. Extend Common Ground
2. Clearing Roadblocks

3. Working with Consensus

1. Extend Common Ground – This Strategy emphasizes points where opposing parties already agree. This is used as a base to expand upon "agreement concerning disagreements about the issues" (Sargent pp1 1988). Initially the focus is on areas of agreement. After the areas of agreement have been identified, areas of disagreement are explored. There is then an agreement about the areas of disagreement.

2. Clearing Roadblocks. – This Strategy deals with the intense conflicts that result for "learned personal or cultural responses" (Sargent pp1 1988) that hide the real issues and concerns. The aware and intentional issues are separated from the "restimulated childhood issues" (Sargent pp1 1988).

3. Working with Consensus - This Strategy identifies synergy which Sargent describes as the "mutual dynamic of group climate and how it controls individual behavior (1988). Methods are provided to enable the Consensus to closely represent the intentions of all parties involved in the conflict.

The above statements are very brief and concise. There is a considerable amount of detail that has been omitted here because this topic could be an entire book in itself.

About Consensus

Consensus is agreement. There is always a consensus in any group or conflict. Initially, the consensus might be that "we're in agreement that we disagree". This phrase, however, is often overused. Frequently opposing parties will say, "Let's agree to disagree". This is okay as a temporary decision. However, disputing parties really need to work through the conflict by using the Strategies and other aspects of the D.C.P. When each opposing party can clearly articulate what the other party wants – this leads to greater understanding and resolution of the conflict.

Synergy – Oftentimes, after opposing parties have worked through the conflict by using the Strategies and various other techniques of the D.C.P. they are able to reach synergy. This is where both parties will actively contribute to a solution and there is a sincere desire to help each other. At this point the attitude is – "how can we make this happen"? "How can we both get what we want"? This is a very different attitude than the initial one when opposing parties first meet each other and attempt to resolve the conflict. With synergy, both parties win. With compromise, both parties usually concede some of their demands. Many of the skills, information and techniques of the D.C.P. that have been discussed are necessary for conflict resolution to work in this manner.

Opposing parties who attempt to resolve a conflict without this knowledge and skills are likely to end up with a compromise (where both parties lose). Sometimes, there is so much hostility and distress among the opposing parties that no resolution can be resolved. However, with consensus and synergy, results can often be achieved that seem unbelievable.

It is interesting to look at how relationships go awry and how this pattern is repeated among groups of people, ranging from two individuals, to a small group to a larger group. Eventually, neighborhoods, towns, cities even nations become involved in conflicts and disputes. Each opposing party brings to the table not only their demands, but their own patterns and distress. However, the patterns and distress that people bring are unaware to both parties. To add to the difficulty of resolving the conflict, parties are often polarized and very distrustful of each other. Oftentimes there is fear that if one really listens to an opposing point of view, one might be tricked into believing it. Unfortunately such an attitude, (based upon fear) only serves to compound the conflict.

When opposing parties get beyond their automatic responses (behavior patterns) and distress, unbelievable results can take place. The role of feelings, thoughts and behavior can not be underestimated in interpersonal relations and in conflict resolution.

It is often necessary for people to "unlearn" such behavior. This topic is addressed in the chapter entitled, "Unlearning".

Here is the "Homework" exercise – which is designed for couples.

The first partner does the following after it is decided who is going first. A coin toss can be used to make this determination. After you've decided who is going first:

1. Do some self validation, identifying your positive qualities. Remember, no "qualifiers" are allowed.

2. Validate your partner- say aloud what you appreciate about your partner

3. Validate the relationship – what you appreciate about the relationship

Now, the other partner has a turn:

1. Do some self validation

2. Validate your partner

3. Validate the relationship

This exercise can be quite effective at improving the relationship you have with each other. In times of stress both partners are likely to temporarily forget what they appreciate about each other, the relationship and themselves. Recall that distress distorts perception, impairs thinking and triggers automatic responses (habits). These earlier learned behaviors can raise havoc with any relationship. By focusing on appreciation of oneself, on one's partner and the relationship, access can be made to Intentional behavior and both partners can relate to each other on a person to person level, rather than as a parent/child level. In essence, both partners will be relating to each other from "ME" to "ME".

Self validation and other skills used in this chapter are described in more detail in the next chapter on Co-Counseling.

Chapter 6 - Co Counseling

Tom Sargent incorporated several "co-counseling" techniques into his material, which will be described a bit later. First, however, I will provide a brief history of how it all began.

The History of Co-Counseling

Initially, L. Ron Hubbard wrote the book, <u>Dianetics</u>. Along came Harvey Jackins, who ran a counseling center at the time in Seattle, Washington who watered down Hubbard's material and created what he called, "Re-evaluation Counseling" or "Co-Counseling." Also known as "RC". Much of Jackins' theory was based upon Hubbard's work. Essentially, Jackins' theory was that we get distressed and store these distress feelings. Re-evaluation Counseling was a peer-counseling program where the Counselor helped the Client to "discharge" – release uncomfortable feelings. After doing so, the client would feel "clear" and could re-evaluate his or her situation.

Tom and Dency Sargent of CT. USA and John Heron from the UK became principle trainers for Jackins. However it wasn't long before all three of these trainers began to have some difficulty with Jackins' autocratic rules and some of this theory and were kicked out of RC. Much to the chagrin of Jackins, these three trainers formed their own version of Co-Counseling, which eventually became known as Co-Counseling International, with local communities in US and in Europe. Central Connecticut in the USA continues to be a hub for co-counseling, which is not affiliated with Jackins.

The rivalry between these two groups continues today with most of it coming from the RC communities that will not allow anyone affiliated with CCI to be a part of their communities or attend a workshop. John Heron had much to say about Jackins' Co-Counseling and the reader is directed to the following website for further information: http://co-cornucopia.org.uk/coco/articles/commun01.htm and http://co-cornucopia.org.uk/coco/articles/dialogue Dency - John Heron.html.

Sargent introduced the idea of "Celebration" into co-counseling – celebration of self (validations for strength) as well as celebration of feelings. While the focus of Jackins' work was always for discharge, Sargent also focused on strength – and introduced some of his Celebrate ME material.

A master at designing workshops and highly effective as a trainer, Sargent introduced co-counseling techniques into his training, which proved highly successful. Sargent would have participants actually practice a technique by using the co-counseling format where one person would act as "speaker" and the other as "listener". Then they would switch roles. For example, frequently within the training of the D.C.P., people would engage in stress reducing techniques, such as a minute of identifying some "new and good" experiences, "ways I'm special" (self esteem) and "times or places I felt relaxed". Such exercises proved to be highly effective and generated a good deal of discussion afterwards. The co-counseling format became a frequent part of the D.C.P. training. However, a separate Co-Counseling class was offered which was taught by Dency Sargent and others for many years. Dency is still listed on the CCI USA website (www.cci-usa.org) as contact person and teacher for CCI USA.

Jackins built an empire of co-counseling communities across the US and in Europe and none of Sargent's people were allowed to participate in any of the RC classes or workshops. According to Sargent who was friendly with one of Jackin's teachers, invited this individual to come to one of his (Sargent's) workshop). The RC teacher agreed. According to Sargent, when Jackins found out he threatened to excommunicate this RC Instructor. The RC Instructor led the workshop for Sargent and was later banned from all RC events and not allowed to teach for any RC community. He eventually formed his own community. This story demonstrates the fierce rivalry that existed between Jackins and Sargent. To this day, the two communities, RC and CCI are separate distinct entities. CCI had a policy of allowing RC'ers to attend their classes and workshops. However, the reverse is not true. To learn more about the distinction between the two organizations, see: http://en.wikipedia.org/wiki/Re-evaluation_Counseling.

It must be emphasized that Sargent adapted many of the RC techniques for training purposes, which proved highly effective. The Designed Change Process did not specifically offer "Co-Counseling Classes". However, co-counseling classes were offered via Change Agents and there are a number of CCI co-counselors and teachers in central Connecticut that still exist today who offer classes and workshops. One of the major differences between the two organizations is the Jackins' organization is hierarchical and focuses nearly exclusively on discharge, while the CCI organization is non-hierarchical and also include focusing upon enhancing self esteem (ME) in addition to discharge. RC counselors were not considered successful unless they could lead their clients to discharging of distress feelings. This could take a variety of forms including laughter, shaking, crying or whatever the client needs to do to release the feeling

The process of sharing time with one person acting as a speaker and the other as a listener, then switching roles became a valuable training technique. This process enables participants to become familiar with specific techniques, practice them and develop proficiency. By using the process in this adapted format, the emphasis is on skills development rather than on discharging (releasing) uncomfortable feelings.

Restrictions

Initially, Jackins issued a set of instructions that restricted co-counselors from socializing with other co-counselors. While there is some merit in making a distinction, Co- Counseling International (initially a local community based in Hartford, CT, led by Tom and Dency Sargent, called People's Re-evaluation Counseling or PRC for short), found these instructions to be too restrictive. Originally, these instructions were written on "blue pages" and have since been referred to as the "Blue Pages.

Jackins had much to say about socializing and romantic relationships developing from co-counseling. In a word, such actions were forbidden.

One of reasons for forbidding co counselors to socialize was Jackin's theory of "Frozen Needs". Jackins theorized that we all have frozen needs, especially to be loved and the closeness created by the co-counseling relationship could result in people thinking that they were in love with each other. (Jackins) One of the unique aspects of the co-counseling relationship is that each person is listened to, rather intensely. We rarely receive that kind of attention. In fact, a counselor is supposed to give his or her "loving, caring attention" (Jackins), which sometimes can be mistaken for romantic love.

Another reason for forbidding co-counselors to socialize is there is a high probability that one might inadvertently violate confidentiality and "re-stimulate" each other. The co-counseling session is completely confidential. Whatever is said or whatever happens is to remain in the session and be strictly confidential. However, after a session, if co-counselors socialize, there is the potential for one to accidentally bring up a topic that was worked on during a counseling session. If this happens the person who worked on this material may become "re-stimulated". This means that they might experience the distress associated with that topic.

Co-counseling International, which developed out of People's Reevaluation Counseling (PRC), does allow co-counselors to socialize, but does encourage a clear distinction between when one is counseling and when one is socializing. There are a number of differences between the two organizations – Jackins' Re-Evaluation Co-Counseling also called RC or Co-Counseling and Co-Counseling International (CCI), of which Sargent was one of the three founders.

CCI does permit socializing, has non-hierarchical structure to its organization and includes validation of self for strength, not just for discharge. (This will be explained a bit later). CCI does not restrict the use of other disciplines and techniques and will allow a member of Jackins' group to enroll in classes and workshop. The reverse is not true about Jackin's organization.

What is Co-Counselingand How Do You Do It?

Co-counseling is a process where two people share time equally as client and as counselor. It is the client who is in charge of the session and tells the counselor what he or she wants. The counselor's primary job is to listen very attentively to the client, unless otherwise directed.

The primary purpose of Co-Counseling to gain clarity by releasing distress, (called discharging). Jacking theorized that if one discharged long enough, one could become clear of all stored distressed feelings and change behavior patterns. The process offers several different types of techniques to promote discharge. Discharge includes, crying, shaking, trembling, laughing, non-repetitive talking, yelling, moaning, screaming and anything else that will naturally allow the body to release distressed feelings. The counselor provides loving, caring attention and generates safety by doing so. When the distress becomes intense enough, the client will discharge.

The Techniques

There are a number of techniques used to promote discharge. These techniques are designed to focus on the distress and intensify it, leading to discharge.

Scanning - A specific type of distressed is focused upon. For example, the client might scan all the times or places they've ever felt sad. By focusing on sad experiences, the client will begin to feel even more sadness which will eventually lead to tears.

"What's on Top" – This technique has the client focus on what they are currently feeling or thinking about. There is often distress attached to it. Having identified the distress, the counselor would encourage the client to focus on it and intensify the distress until discharge occurs.

Direction Setting and Holding – a Direction is a statement or phrase designed to produce discharge. It is often the exact opposite of what the client is experiencing. "Holding the Direction" means repeating the Direction over and over again until discharge results. Oftentimes hardy laughter results from saying a Direction and what is amazing is the Direction will be instantly forgotten by the client. For example, if a client felt pressured and anxious due to time constraints and had a lot to do, the client might say as a Direction – "I have all the time in the world", or "I have nothing to do". The counselor would encourage the client t say this statement with passion and might even ask the client to stand up, smile and say the direction in a loud, passionate voice. This oftentimes results in laughter by the client and sometimes the client isn't even able to say the direction. With time the client will be able to say the Direction, releasing the distress.

Non-Repetitive Talking – Using this technique, the client talks about a distressing experience, with the counselor encouraging the client to discharge in the telling of the story.

Pillow Pounding – This is a particular technique designed to release anger. The client hits a pillow and yells, "I'm angry". Oftentimes, after several repetitions of pounding the pillow and saying, "I'm angry", the client actually discharges some anger.

Validation – This technique has the client state a positive quality about him that leads to discharge. It often is a positive statement that the client initially might not believe. Some examples include, "I'm beautify, "I'm sexy", "I'm intelligent". The client keeps repeating the positive quality. This technique is similar to Direction Holding, except the client keeps saying a positive quality again and again, with the help of the counselor. The counselor may ask the client to say the validation again, with a stronger voice or more passionately. The client may be asked to stand up and say the validation again. He or she may be told to "say it like you mean it"

Non-Discharging Techniques – These techniques are designed to move the client out of distress and into clarity or "present time". In fact, there is a technique called, "Present Time" that has the client focus on the here and now. Some examples include, asking the client to say the days of the week, and then say them backwards. Ask the client to find 5 objects that have the color blue. Ask questions of common knowledge is another favorite – such as naming the months of the year, or 4 cities beginning with the letter "C" or whatever letter the counselor chooses.

New and Good – This technique, which has been described in a previous chapter can be used either at the beginning of a session (traditionally) or at the end. If the client is able to identify a New and Good, the client is back in "present time."

Sargent introduced the idea of using Validation for strength. Rather than focusing on discharge, he would have the client repeat the validation for strength and perhaps scan ways to support the idea that it is true. For example, if a client was working on being intelligent, the client might be asked to scan all the times that he or she acted intelligently, and then say the validation again. This was part of the larger idea of "Celebration" that Sargent introduced to Co-Counseling. The idea of Celebration was discussed in Chapter Three.

About Sessions and Classes

A session can last from a few minutes to an hour or even longer. The key thing to remember is that the time must be divided equally. If I take 15 minutes, you take 15 minutes. If however, a counselor can't keep the attention, that people must stop the session and inform the person that they can't sustain the attention. The usual expression that is used is "I can't be there for you". There are other circumstances when a counselor needs to stop a session. Another example is when a counselor begins to experience his or her own distress – to the point that they become "re-stimulated". Again, if this happens, the counselor needs to stop the session. Usually it is best for both counselor and client to do some New and Goods and some Present Time. Then they would need to renegotiate how long they are going to counselor, which is called negotiating a contract.

Classes are taught by teachers trained in Co-counseling. Classes generally run for 6-8 weeks at a time, meeting once a week. Each class consists of both theory and application. A student can expect to actually do some co-counseling during the session. Usually, after a new technique is demonstrated, people select partners and practice the technique. It is also expected and required that each person in the class will have at least one counseling session outside of class with a classmate. Beginners are advised to start with a small amount of time at first, then progress to longer times. An initial session might be for 10 or 15 minutes, each. To help students, they are often given a format of what to do regarding the techniques.

For example, after deciding how long you will counsel and who is going first, the client might begin with some New and Goods. The next item might be to do some scanning of a particular distressed feeling. This would lead to focusing upon the feeling and intensifying it until the client discharges. With new students, discharge is not always achieved during the first session. The amount of safety and attention the counselor can provide is crucial to helping the client to discharge. If difficulties arise, students are encouraged to bring them up for discussion at the class – focusing on the technique, not the contents.

Non - Content Co-counseling – In co-counseling it is quite possible to counselor someone who is focusing 100% on their feelings and not on the content. You, as a counselor do not even need to know or understand any of the content. You might have a client crying for 15 minutes and never says a word of content. The job of the counselor is to promote discharge, not necessarily to understand or even know the content. I in fact, have counseled with people from foreign countries who speak in their native tongue during the session. I had no idea what they were saying, but I was able to provide caring attention that resulted in them discharging the distressed feeling. It should be noted that this is very different from the traditional role of a counselor. Again, it should be emphasized that it is the client who is in charge of the session, not the counselor. People who are professional counselors often have difficulty with this.

A Touchy Subject

Oftentimes counselor and client hold hands or maintain some physical contact. This is useful for the counselor because you can detect all sorts of information about the client – hand tension, hands going cold, indicating fear, etc. It is also useful for the client because it can provide safety. However, some people don't like the idea of holding hands or touching each other and that needs to be respected. Sometimes the holding of hands can serve as a way of anchoring the distress. If the client is discharging and at that moment the counselor squeezes the clients hands, there can be a strong association established and when these two people counsel again, if the counselor squeezes the client's hand with the same amount of pressure, the counselor can trigger the emotion/feeling that client had previously. This is called "Anchoring" and is a Neuro-Linguistic Programming technique the Co-Counseling Community either doesn't seem to be aware that it can happen or isn't too concerned about it.

If a client has an issue with touching or physical contact, he or she might choose to work on that issue. But, if the client doesn't want to hold hands, the counselor must respect it. Sometimes two males counseling each other will have a problem with hand holding – possibly a homophobic reaction. While these can be excellent issues to work on, one must remember that it is the client that is in charge of the session and determines what will take place, what will be worked on and what if anything the counselor needs to do.

Another manner of touching, which can be problematic to some people is hugging. Frequently, after having a session, the client and counselor will hug each other. Usually the counselor will ask if the client wants a hug. Sometimes the client will ask for a hug. While hugging is quite common in co-counseling, occasionally a person may not wish to be hugged. An individual's request to refrain from hugging must be respected. While such a topic might be an excellent issue for counseling, it is up to client to choose whether or not he/she wishes to work on that issue.

Workshops

Periodically, teacher and communities may offer workshops. These can range for a few hours to an entire weekend. Once a year CCI USA offers an International Workshop, usually in early April. This workshop generally lasts for 5 days and is often attended by some co-counselors from some European Communities. However, the majority of co-counselors are from the US and a majority from Connecticut, which still serves as a hub for co-counseling in the US. In Europe, most countries have their own communities. The European Communities offer an annual CCI International Workshop as well. In addition, individual communities in various countries may host their own workshops which are open to both Europeans and Americans.

Looking over the various techniques that Sargent used in his Designed Change Process, one can recognize several co-counseling techniques that he adapted. Some include the use of New and Goods, Scanning, Direction Holding and Present Time. The adaption of these techniques proved to be highly effective in training as has been discussed earlier.

While co-counseling continues to exist, the D.C.P. was dormant until this book. As the reader can see, co – counseling plays a major role in the D.C.P. It is interesting to note that Sargent himself, did attend annual CCI workshops, but did not specifically teach co-counseling classes. He incorporated the co-counseling techniques into his work which he eventually called the Designed Change Process. It was his wife Dency Sargent who played a major role in the co-counseling community by teaching co-counselors and training teachers. Dency is still listed on the CCI USA web site a contact person.

The Role of Co-Counseling Techniques in Stress Management

A number of co-counseling techniques can be used in stress management and I have incorporated many of them.

New and Goods – I always begin workshops with this technique. It moves participants away from distress and has them focus on something positive. It is a good stress reducer that is easy to do.

Scanning is particularly useful for working with feelings. To intensify any feeling, all you have to do is focus on it. The scanning technique provides you with a way of doing this. As discussed earlier, there are several other uses of the scanning technique. It can be used to scan both positive and negative feelings as well as patterns. It can also be used to strengthen validations as was discussed earlier.

The Interrupter – This is an enhanced version of the Direction Holding technique that consists of three steps:

1. Identify the pattern or feeling you wish to change.

2. State the exact opposite – example, "I'm so busy" becomes "I've all the time in the world".

3. Continue saying your Interrupter until you discharge the distress feeling(s).

Note: a good Interrupter will often produce hardly laughter. At first you might be resistant to say your Interrupter. If you have any feelings about saying your Interrupter, it is probably a good one. Write it down because you will immediately forget it, even if you've been working on it for 15 minutes or longer. After you have discharged the distress feeling, you may wish to use another technique, depending upon your Interrupter. For example, if you were saying "I am very punctual person" (as an Interrupter), at some point you might wish to scan times that you did arrive on time.

The Interrupter is a powerful technique that can be used to interrupt either a feeling or a behavior pattern. The key is to practice your Interrupter. Keep saying it. Initially, you may feel resistant. After a brief period of time working on it, you will probably discharge. Continue working until the discharge stops. By "working", I mean keep saying your Interrupter. You may want to have your counselor encourage you to continue working on it by having them say things such as "again", or "keep going" or "what is your Interrupter"?

Resources for Co-Counseling

First of all, it should be clear that there are two major organizations – Jackin's Co-Counseling, (also known as Re-Evaluation Counseling) and Co-Counseling International (CCI). The later organization consists of CCI Europe and CCI USA.

Here are some useful web sites about Co-Counseling:

CCI- World News Service - http://www.cciwns.com/ (Niek Sickenga, Editor)

CCI USA - http://cci-usa.org/index_2.htm

CCI Europe (UK)

http://www.co-cornucopia.org.uk/coco/literature.htm

History of CCI

http://www.cciwns.com/cciwns.com/index.php/theory-and-culture/theory/history-of-cci

Brief history of RC by Wikipedia

http://en.wikipedia.org/wiki/Re-evaluation_Counseling

Re-Evaluation Counseling -http://www.rc.org/.

Jackins has written numerous books about Co-counseling and Re-Evaluation Counseling has it's publisher called Rational Island, http://www.rationalisland.com/.

For the history and general information about CCI

http://en.wikipedia.org/wiki/Co-Counselling_International#History

Several books and other literature have been written by CCI. Niek Sickenga, who edits CCI Work New Service has archives on CCI and would be a good person to contact for information about books written by CCI authors.

While co-counseling is a separate organization with its own history and protocol, Sargent adapted various techniques into the D.C.P. As has been previously stated, these techniques proved to be a highly effective way to train people. The combination of various techniques proved to be even more effective. It should be noted that Sargent didn't necessarily use the Co-Counseling techniques for discharge purposes. Rather, he used them for strength. For example, if Sargent was working with someone to enhance self esteem, he might have them use the Scanning technique and scan all the times, places or ways they have used a specific quality.

Here is an example, which also serves as a specific exercise. Say the following: "I am an intelligent person". Now identify, what feeling do you feel and/or what thought. For many people, they will say, "I'm not intelligent" or they will feel embarrassment or hurt or some other distress feeling. The next step would be to scan all the times, places or ways that you have been intelligent. Having done that, go back and again say, "I'm an intelligent person". Notice how you feel less distress saying it and the sentence begins to seem like it is true.

It is this unique use of various co-counseling techniques adapted to promote strength (self- esteem) that make the D.C.P. so effective. The same techniques are used in Co-Counseling but for a different purpose – namely, to promote the release of uncomfortable feelings (discharge).

The very concept of using Validation for strength, which Sargent introduced to Co-Counseling, was a somewhat radical departure from the Jackins' style of Co-Counseling. In Jackin's style Co-Counseling, one would say a validation (a positive statement or quality about oneself, for the purpose of discharging. Sargent introduced what he called Celebration, where a person would still use Validation, but not necessarily for discharging, but rather for strength. This concept was adapted into the D.C.P. and again, proved to be highly effective. How can someone improve one's sense of self esteem? Have them celebrate their ME – validate oneself for strength. If the validation (positive quality) doesn't seem real or strong, then the scanning technique would be utilized.

The ability to experience a strong sense of self esteem is crucial in order to access Intentional behavior. It is also of paramount importance to understand that once one is drawn into Automatic behavior, especially as the result of

108

distress, access to Intentional behavior and especially to one's ME is difficult, if not impossible, without specialized training in the D.C.P. It is for this reason that such an emphasis was placed on one's ability to create and build a solid sense of self (esteem).

Many therapists have benefited from this knowledge and set of skills immensely. Using traditional training, it is very difficult to get a client to see their positive qualities. Even if they are told by others, the client will usually resist or refute any validations. But using the D.C.P. people learn about "invalidations" and how patterns perpetuate negative beliefs. By using the various adapted co-counseling techniques people are quickly able to improve their sense of self esteem. If there is a lot of distress feeling attached to doing this, then discharge proves to be quit useful.

Summary

Co-counseling is a peer-facilitated process where two people share time equally as client and counselor. The client is in charge of the session and the counselor's role is to provide attention and help the client if directed. Various techniques are used to bring about the release of uncomfortable feelings. The releasing of these feelings is called "discharge". In addition to counseling for discharge, Sargent introduced the idea of counseling for strength and further adapted a variety of co-counseling skills into the D.C.P. which has proven to be highly effective.

Jackins, who started Co-Counseling (Re-Evaluation Counseling) based it upon L. Ron Hubbard's book, Dianetics. John Heron, Dency and Tom Sargent were originally co-counselors for Jackins and were kicked out of his organization. The three went on to form their own version of Co-Counseling, now known as Co-Counseling International, CCI with a USA organization and a

European Organization. Sargent introduced some non-discharging techniques to CCI and eventually further adapted them into the D.C.P..

These techniques proved highly effect for training purposes.

I have adapted these techniques for use in Stress Management that have also proved to be highly effective. Many of the techniques discussed in this chapter are essential for use in Unlearning, which will be discussed in the next chapter.

A Model for Co-Counseling

The following is a suggested model for co-counseling. First, decide who is going first and how much time you want. Remember that the time must be shared equally. If you take 15 minutes, your partner takes 15 minutes. The first time you co-counsel start with 10 or 15 minutes. When you are the counselor, you must focus 100% on your client and provide loving, caring attention. If you are not able to do this, either select a shorter duration of time, or you go first. If both people are distressed, each of you can do some New and Goods, first.

1. Begin with some New and Goods

2. If you already are in contact with a distressed feeling, focus on that and say aloud how you feel. Example, "I feel angry" or "I am angry" (Say it in a loud angry voice. Your counselor can encourage you by instructing you to say it LOUDER!

3. If you are not in contact with any distressed feeling, do some scanning. Pick an uncomfortable feeling, such as hurt, fear or angry and scan all the times, places or ways you have experienced this feeling

4. Next, refer to item #2. Keep saying how you feel and intensify the feeling

5. Do a few self validations. If there is distress connected to any validation, allow the distress to intensify and discharge it.

When the balance of intensity of feeling and level of safety is balanced properly, you will automatically discharge the feeling (release it). Recall that there are many different forms of discharge (laughing, crying, shaking, yelling, non-repetitive talking, etc.)

6. Near the end of your session, begin moving into "Present Time" – focus on non-distressing items. Pay attention to details in the room. Have your co-counselor ask you "present time" questions, such as name all the items in the room that are of a certain color (for example, the color brown). Questions of common knowledge are good to ask – such as name the days of the week, the months of a year.

Note: The above items are only suggestions. You might choose to just do one of them for your entire session.

7. As the counselor, make sure your client is back in "present time" and no longer focusing on distress. It is often a good idea for both of you to physically stand up and walk around the room a bit. Sometimes the client may want to be hugged.

8. Reverse roles and begin the whole process again.

As has been previously discussed, many of the co-counseling techniques have been incorporated into the Designed Change Process as training techniques. The next chapter discusses these and other techniques which are required for "Unlearning".

Chapter 7 - Unlearning

The Designed Change Process is a compilation of strategies that are effective for intentional change in human life (Sargent. 85, 1984). The strategies are combinations of various parts of the bimodal model developed and designed to bring about change in human situations. "The strategies integrated together <u>are</u> the Designed Change Process"

(Sargent. 85, 1984).

Examples of the Strategies:

1. Self Confidence – often results from experience and a clear understanding of one's personal qualities and capabilities. Self confidence can be enhanced by the D.C.P. Sargent identifies that "… confidence is easily confused with defensive overconfidence…" (86). Bragging or acting "macho" are examples and "… are defensive reactions to feelings of inadequacy" (86). The person who is highly skilled and recognizes his/her skills and abilities has no need to brag or boast. Oftentimes such individuals act in a humble manner. However, defensive overconfidence often increases when an individual recognizes a gap between the demands of a situation and his/her real capabilities. In such a situation, an individual will brag or boast of their knowledge. Ironically, a truly confident person might probably admit that they simply don't know and will recognize not knowing a specific bit of information does not lessen their confidence.

Self confidence varies from situation to situation. However, over self confidence is brought about by distress. As an individual begins to recognize that the situation is demanding more than what one is capable of doing, distress occurs, which results in automatic behavior. This can have dangerous results because once the Automatic mode of behavior is triggered, Intentional behavior in no longer accessible.

2. Increasing Awareness. Although we might believe that we are aware of everything we do, the fact is a great deal of our behavior is UNAWARE! Recall that in the Automatic mode of behavior, we are not aware. Human behavior is so complex that it is not possible to be aware of every single thing we do. However, any behavior can be brought into our awareness by deliberate attention and with the help of someone trained in the D.C.P..

Awareness is the key to any type of personal change. If we are not aware of what we are doing we can't change until we become aware. Intentional behavior can be brought about by paying attention to the relationship between feelings and behavior. The sequence of events must be slowed down and careful attention must be paid to one step at a time.

"Awareness as a strategy brings unaware to intentional control. It is most effective for unwanted behavior patterns and watching how they operate in times of distress. Once we have become aware of the hidden dynamics of unwanted behavior, it is easier to change." (Sargent. 88 1984)

3. From Past to Present – Distress can stimulate intense patterns and memories from the past that seem as if they are coming from the present. It can be nearly impossible to distinguish between the two. Am I feeling this way because of the current

situation or am I feeling this way because of the past – a restimulation of the past? It is necessary to clarify the difference in order to respond accurately and appropriately.

"A sense of being overwhelmed and powerless is one clue which indicates that pasts feelings have taken over" (Sargent. 88 1984). Sargent (1984) claims that this is most common in interpersonal relations. Feelings from the past are attributed to the present and we are not trained to know the difference. The result is the individual often ends up fighting past struggles with present partners. (Sargent 1984). How does one tell the difference? According to Sargent (1984), feelings from the past are very strong and overwhelming. They trigger automatic behaviors resulting in outdated and inappropriate actions.

The strategy to deal with this problem involves an intense focus on the present situation. "Refocusing attention to the physical seems to be more effective than fixing on thoughts and feelings and then attempting to resolve the stress they represent" (Sargent pp 91, 1984).

One needs to learn to dwell on the other individual and pay close attention so that the intensities of the restimulation come to pass. This strategy is considered a very intensive and active awareness exercise combined with a concentrated shift in focus (Sargent 1984). This is an important strategy because there is frequently confusion between past and present feelings in interpersonal relations.

4. Relaxation and Meditation are used in the D.C.P. as a method of exploring the self. Self appreciation ("ME") exercises are repeated as a number of built in associations are established. Participants identify appreciated characteristics and write them down later after the exercise is completed (See Special Place).

A similar exercise is used to create an intense (energized) experience, rather than a relaxing one. Participants stand and do some centering exercises and stimulating music is played, designed to excite, rather than relax. The same associations are used, where participants touch part of their Special Place and note appreciations of self ("ME").

5. Shift in Focus – Participants learn to shift focus in two areas: 1) the focus on feelings and stress and 2) the focus from various perspectives. Many of the stress management techniques or management of feeling techniques are focusing. Any feeling will intensify if one focuses upon it. By combining with other techniques, such as scanning, participants learn how to change their feelings by focusing upon different feelings. Oftentimes when feelings change, behavior changes as well, especially if the feeling is a distress feeling. In addition, the perception about the situation will change as the feeling changes. Recall that distress distorts perception. By combining a change in feelings and perspective, behavior can be changed as well.

What a person's feelings will be can be determined by one's focus of attention. If one focuses upon distress, one experiences distress. If one focuses on pleasure, one experiences pleasure. While these statements may appear to be obvious and simplistic, one must learn how to focus and shift one's focus. The scanning technique is one of several that can be used. It's important to realize that external events and memories stored in the brain can produce whatever feelings the person associates with them (Sargent 1984). Distress feelings seem to attract attention and oftentimes people spend a lot of time in distress. However, a shift in focus can result in pleasurable feelings and numerous techniques for changing feelings were presented in the chapter on Feelings.

File Carding – This is a technique that Sargent took directly from Alcoholics Anonymous. According to Sargent, alcoholics collect resentments to increase their level of feelings (distress) in order to justify a drink. When the stress becomes intolerable the alcoholic can drink. Resentment collecting is a deliberate type of scanning where all sources: past, present and future are scanned for resentment. It is like a file card index of all sources of various feelings and file cards for resentment are pulled.

This is pretty easy to do. Identify an unpleasant feeling you want to feel. Then remember all the people who made you feel that way. It won't take long for your feeling to intensify. You can do this with any feeling, pleasant or unpleasant. All of us have file card feelings. You can use this method to intensify any feeling.

Alcoholics Anonymous invented a way of interrupting the file carding process. They call the collection of resentments "stinkin' thinkin'" with a little laughter (Sargent 1984). They build an association between the file carding and the laughter. The laughter and the resentment are incompatible. This idea has been developed within the D.C.P. in a couple of ways. One is the idea of interrupting distress that was discussed in the chapter on Feelings. However, another variation on theme involves participants to visualize actual file cards, where there is room to write on each card. Pleasant associations of feelings can be written on the cards and unpleasant ones can be interrupted. Some participants in the D.C.P. use the phrase "stinkin' thinkin" to identify when they are using a filing card system of collecting unpleasant feelings. Often the statement, "Oh, I'm doing that "stinkin'feelin' stuff again" is enough to interrupt the file card system or at the least, draw attention to it.

6. Desensitization – consists of reducing a person's sensitivity to stimulus. This is done by repeatedly exposing the individual to the stimulation (stress). Many years ago, there was a sexuality workshop done at Change Agents, the building where Tom conducted trainings. The participants were desensitized by displaying a picture of a sexual organ on an overhead projector. Participants were asked to call out every slang name they could think of for each body part. Each slang name was written on newsprint. At first there was a lot of giggling and laughter and people were a bit hesitant to call out a slang name. However after awhile, they became desensitized and believe it or not, the exercise eventually became boring. How many dirty words and can you label a sexual organ before it loses its effect? After going through all the female and male sex organs, with this process, the participants became desensitized. Then they could talk about sexual matters without distress and information could be presented to them without them experiencing distress.

Both stress and the meaning of the stress can be desensitized as the above paragraph has demonstrated. It is interesting to note that after desensitization, the physiological events of a feeling may still be present, but they don't elicit the same response as they previously did (Sargent 1984).

Desensitization can be applied to a variety of settings. It is used in therapy especially working with clients who have fears or phobias. The military also uses it in training soldiers. Many other professions find it quite useful including any profession where there is likely to be a high level of distress.

7. Incompatibility – Recall that pain and pleasure are incompatible. Many compatibilities can be used within the dynamics of human behavior to block undesirable responses. Focusing more specifically on pain and pleasure, this could also include depression and anger, fear and anger, anxiety and intentionality (Sargent 1984). Sometimes these incompatibilities actually block intentional behavior, such as distress inhibiting Intentional behavior.

There are several feelings that are incompatible with each other. According to Sargent, "... the physiology of fear is incompatible with anger and excitement is incompatible with depression" (Sargent pp 100, 1984). Because excitement is incompatible with depression, an individual must work very hard not to get excited in order to keep the depression going. Excitement can also be generated by running or some other physical exercise. Feelings of fear, depression, loneliness and guilt can all be altered by focusing on anger. Ironically, anger is often the cause of depression, but instead of expressing it, the individual suppresses it and becomes depressed. (Sargent 1984).

Besides the physiological incompatibilities, there are an untold number of incompatible associations that are incompatible with each other. While the incompatible associations of one person may not match those of another, they are fixed and predictable in any one person (Sargent 1984). A person's tone of voice, facial expressions and body posture all have feelings associated with them. Unwanted feelings (distress) can be changed by changing any of these traits to an association with an incompatible feeling. For example, changing an angry tone to a silly tone is incompatible with anger. Doing so weakens the anger. Imagine expressing anger in a silly tone of voice, such as a high squeaky voice like one is imitating a cartoon character or one of the Muppets, such as Miss Piggy. Try it sometime when you're angry. The action is incompatible with anger. Another example would be to try maintaining a depression and putting a big smile or silly grin on your face.

Incompatibility can be used to change a number of attitudes, behaviors and feelings. Ironically, oftentimes when participants use the Direction Holding technique, their behavior, posture, facial expressions are often incompatible with what they are saying. A participant might say I'm angry, but will say it in a mousy voice, or almost a whisper. It should be noted that in this particular instant the participant is actually trying to intensify the anger. However, if one were actually angry and wanted to diffuse the anger, one's posture, facial expressions, tone of voice and volume of voice could be used in a manner incompatible with anger.

There are many situations where feelings, behaviors and attitudes can be altered by using this technique of incompatibility. However, it can be taken one step further. The incompatibility between the associated feeling or behavior can be associated. With practice one can strengthen the association to the point that this association of incompatible feeling and behavior can be actually used to disrupt the undesired behavior automatically in times of stress. Rather than the behavior being automatically tripped by the distress (like someone flips a switch), the individual automatically interrupts the undesired behavior. This is a very powerful strategy and quite fun to do once it is learned.

8. Laughter – deserves special attention because it is a highly effective way to change feelings. Recall that in Co-Counseling, laughter is considered a form of discharge – which releases uncomfortable (distress)

feelings. Physiologically, laughter is incompatible with stress and laughter usually occurs outside of behavior patterns. Many people who are depressed or angry will refuse to interrupt this experience with laughter, because they know that laughter is incompatible with depression or anger and doing so will cause them to feel less angry or depressed. You can ruin a good depression or bout of anger by laughing, so the individual will resist laughing. Norman Cousins, in his book, <u>The Anatomy of an Illness</u>, literally laughed himself to good health and described how he did this.

One quality that separates humans from other animals is our ability to laugh. In order to laugh, we must step outside of ourselves and see the contradictions that surround us (Sargent 1984). "The ability to become objective through laugher is one of the human organism's [sic] for interrupting unwanted behavior" (Sargent. 102, 1984). It has long been know by people of various professions that laughter is a release. Good comedians do a real service when they get an audience to laugh. Oftentimes trainers will tell a humorous story to "break the ice" and lower participants' stress level. When we laugh, with the exception of embarrassment or derisive laughter, we are oftentimes releasing distress. There are some people who believe that laughter massages our internal organs and that a good 'belly laugh' can do wonders. At the time of this printing, more and more Yoga teachers are including laughter as a specific type of Yoga. Laughter is an effective strategy used in the D.C.P..

9. Self Modification – is the use of various behavioral change techniques used by the individual as opposed to someone attempting to change the individual, such as a therapist, "as it is commonly done" (Sargent. 102, 1984).

120

"After the unwanted behavior pattern has been identified, methods of interrupting it are explored, and desired behavior patterns to replace the unwanted ones are developed." (Sargent. 102, 1984). This is an essential part of the D.C.P.. The unwanted behavior is interrupted and replaced with a new behavior. However, both the unwanted behavior and the new behavior are integrated so that when the old behavior starts to run, it is immediately interrupted and replaced automatically (Sargent 1984). To accomplish this, an individual must practice interrupting the old behavior and replacing it with the new behavior. This is done by building associations.

The first step of self modification is to identify an unwanted behavior. This is usually quite easy to do as most people are aware of something they do that they would like to change. The next step involves interrupting the unwanted behavior. This is often accomplished by focusing on distress feelings that trigger the behavior. Those feelings can be interrupted using a variety of techniques. The use of incompatibility is one method that can be used, but there are several others.

Once the behavior has been interrupted, a new behavior must be put into place. This is a mistake that some co-counselors make. They discharge and interrupt the old behavior pattern, but they fail to replace it with new one.

If a new behavior isn't utilized, the old behavior will continue to run. The two behaviors are integrated so when the old behavior runs, it is immediately interrupted and replaced with the new behavior. The earlier discussion about 'associations' comes into play here.

The end result is a new behavior that replaces the old one. It should be emphasized that once a participant has the information and skills the individual intentionally changes himself or herself, unlike other disciplines where an outside person, such as therapist attempts to change the individual. Thus self modification is truly self modification. The D.C.P. seeks to teach or train individuals how to make their own changes. Other unwanted behaviors can be interrupted and replaced. It is also important to note that self modification uses both Intentional and Automatic behavior and that the Process validates the self – meaning it assures the individual that change can be self induced. In order to use this Process, one must have a solid sense of self ("ME"), which is why an emphasis is place on the development of "ME" in all aspects of Designed Change Process training.

10. Training the Brain – Recall that there are two types of behavior: Intentional and Automatic. Intentional behavior requires deliberate attention and repetition until the new behavior is learned. Auto is like a giant hard drive of a computer that has an unlimited storage capacity and responds rapidly. The sequence to learning new behavior is 1) flexible exploration and 2) repeated until the new behavior is recorded into long term memory. Under usual conditions, this sequence works well until a person encounters a situation that requires change. Then, it fails.

Learned responses are automatic and permanent. However, oftentimes when a new situation arises the old responses are inappropriate. Despite the fact that they no longer work, individuals continue to use them anyway. For example, when attempting to cross a busy street, people will push a button on a pole to change the light. But what happens when the light doesn't change. Most people will repeatedly press the button and wait and press the button again and again. Eventually they realize that the button isn't working and that the light won't change by pressing it. In this example, people try the old behavior repeatedly, but eventually are forced to change (until they encounter it again). However, consider the following situation: a young man discovers that if he causes a scene at a store, the clerk will give him what he wants (a refund). He does this at a few other stores and it works there, too. Now the behavior is learned and automatic. Then, one day at a gym, he gets into an argument with the person at the desk and argues and starts to cause a scene. At this point the behavior is automatic. He begins to rant and rave and eventually yell and holler. But he doesn't get what he wants. Yet, he continues with the behavior. He is told by the gym staff that he must leave. But the young man continues the same behavior, even more. Finally, he is warned that if he doesn't leave immediately, they will call the police. He doesn't leave and the police come and escort him out of the building.

The old outdated or inappropriate behavior will continue to run even when it doesn't produce the results desired. Most behavior patterns of this nature are brought about by distress. In this example, the young man was angry. He had learned that if he rants and rave and yells and hollers, he will get what he wants. But, this time he didn't. He continued with the same behavior even though it wasn't getting him anywhere. It nearly got him arrested.

Can you begin to see how disruptive and inappropriate old behavior patterns can be? In this example above, the outdated behavior was triggered by anger. For this individual or for anyone to learn a new behavior, one must also unlearn. Past behavior is recorded permanently and is not forgotten. It's like a chain link fence. You can't break the link, but you can add to a link and thereby change it. However, the old behavior is still there and in times of distress, could resurface.

It is essential to learn how to train the brain for change. In addition to the sequence of exploration and invention, followed by learning and storing, there is an additional step necessary. One must learn a method of interfering with the old behavior. It is not enough to learn a new behavior. The old behavior must be interrupted. What is required is both the interruption of the old behavior and the implementation of the new behavior, which must be practiced repeatedly until it becomes automatic.

Whatever will interrupt the old behavior must be learned and added to the old behavior to make the interruption automatic (Sargent 1984). The new behavior must be practiced and the entire sequence must be practiced as well until it becomes automatic. Because old behavior patterns remain in our brains, the old behavior could still surface if one experiences enough distress.

In order to be effective, one must be flexible, yet able to run automatic behavior when it is appropriate. First responders (fire and medical personnel) are trained to seek out the most serious injured victims. The same is true in an emergency room of a hospital. However, in a crisis, with large numbers of people injured, a different approach is necessary. In such a situation, first responders must make a choice since they can not save everyone. Unfortunately, old learned responses kick in and medical staff attempt to treat people who are so severely injured that they will not survive. Yet, there are other people who are badly injured that could survive if they received immediate treatment. However, sometimes first responders focus on those who are critically injured who have the least probability of survival. It is a judgment call and no one likes to make it. But, once old patterns of behavior kick in, there is no decision making. The behavior runs and people just do as they've learned to do. Tragically, in such a situation, more people may perish than is really necessary.

This example dramatically demonstrates the need to interrupt and replace an old behavior with a new one. This

124

is called Unlearning and is one of the more advanced aspects of the D.C.P.

Unlearning is "eliminating part learned responses through rerouting" (Sargent 1 1987). "Learning to unlearn requires improving the familiarity with the self, and skill with interrupting undesirable behavior" (Sargent pp 85 1984). This is the most advanced application of the D.C.P.. Simply stated – "behaviors which are undesirable in the present context are replaced with a new response" (Sargent 1 1987). This is a complex process and requires use of nearly all aspects of the D.C.P. A person unlearns by attaching new responses which serve to "reroute, inhibit, or arrest the automatic functioning of the original process... (Sargent 1 1987). The "rerouting mechanism is imbedded in the original response sequence ... (1).

A simple way of explaining this is that an undesirable behavior is interrupted and replaced with a new behavior. The undesirable behavior is often one that was learned from the past. However, even earlier learned responses as far aback as childhood can be triggered in times of stress and they automatically run without the individual's awareness. In fact, most of the time an individual will not be aware of an automatic learned response. It is well known that "the earliest learned responses of an individual are those which were useful in relating to significant other ...as a young child" (Sargent 1 1987). The basic parent/child relationship is one that we all experienced. In tines of stress we often revert back to child behavior (learned response) or parent behavior, which in this case is telling someone what to do or what not to do as a parent would say to a child. Child behavior is sometimes referred to as "know nothing" behavior, while parent behavior is sometimes referred to as "know it all" behavior (Sargent 4 1987).

Tragically, these early learned response sneak into our interpersonal relationships. Even worse is that they can occur in complex technological operations resulting in disastrous consequences of such industries as nuclear, medicine, the airline and practically any other industry as well. While many times an automatic response is essential, sometimes it can be disastrous. For example, consider a pilot who flies a particular type of plane and then later is assigned to fly a different type of plane. In times of distress the pilot will automatically resort to a learned response of flying the first plane, even though this action is inappropriate and could even result in a disaster while flying the other plane. This is an example of how Unlearning can be extremely useful.

Based upon the bi-modal model of behavior, which is the essence of the D.C.P., everyone uses two informational processing functions Sargent 1984)

1.   Aware – which is intentional, flexible and creative

2.   Automatic – which is unaware, reliable and rigid.

The Aware function is of "extremely limited capacity" (Sargent 3 1987). The Automatic function is of "immense capacity". In essence, both Aware and Automatic situations are necessary. The difficulty is that the Automatic function is triggered by distress and as its name implies – happens automatically. Therefore, an individual when placed under stress will not have access to the Aware function or even something recently learned. Instead, "whatever automatic response is dominate will determine the present behavior" (Sargent 6 1987).

"Unlearning is the process of permanently interrupting behavior patterns stored in the long term memory of the brain" (Sargent 8 1987). An example of unlearning is when a person drives a new car. A person needs to 'unlearn' the habits of driving new car. A more specific example is someone who switches from a car with an automatic transmission to a stick shift. The process of 'unlearning' requires the addition of new material to the memory" (8) Behavior patterns are like a chain link. The link can not be broken but one can add a link which in effect changes the configuration of the chain. In the case of memory, a pattern can be "reconfigured in order to prevent them from occurring automatically when they are not wanted" (Sargent 8 1987) "Unlearning provides a rerouting of the automatic sequence through a method similar to a "patch" of a computer program (8). If the automatic sequence is re-stimulated it lead to a new behavioral outcome" Once the new behavior is learned it becomes aware- like all learned sequences. "In interpersonal patterns, the experience with the re-stimulated patterns can sometimes be very unpleasant". (Sargent 9 1987) In re-stimulation, the individual experiences the old feeling and behavior pattern usually by some type of association.

Rerouting

There are several steps that are required to unlearn anything. These steps need to be tailored to the exact needs of the individual. The order of these steps will vary from person to person.

Step One – "acknowledge that importance of contriving methods to block the unwanted behavior automatically … ". (Sargent 1 1987) This means one must find ways to block the automatic behavior (pattern) and do so automatically, eventually. This may sound a bit strange – to block automatic behavior automatically. It is also necessary to "identify the behaviors which need to be rerouted" (Sargent 10, 1987).

Step Two – get to know the unwanted behavior …" (Sargent 10 1987). This means being able to recognize it, understand how it works and how it is triggered.

Remember that this behavior is unknown to the individual and it is automatic. Many people think that they can re-experience their unwanted behavior just by thinking about it. This is false. "The only way to become familiar with a pattern is to be inside of it" (Sargent 11 1987). This can be distressing.

Step Three – "select something which will interrupt the unwanted behavior" (Sargent 11 1987). The interrupter often can be a word or phrase that frequently will produce a chuckle or even hearty laughter. The word or phrase can be accompanied by other behaviors such as the tone of voice, posture and a variety of other behaviors.

Step Four – "integrate the entire sequence into everyday life" (Sargent 12 1987). One must not only practice the new behavior and the interrupter. One must practice using the entire sequence – the new behavior in one's life. In this 4th step, the individual stays clear of the past learned responses into the present, where life is no longer disrupted by undesirable behavior, feelings, stress and or thoughts (Sargent 13 1987).

Relearning can be applied to both interpersonal relations and complex technology. It was actually designed by Sargent to be used in complex technology. It has been used extensively in interpersonal relations. "Most individuals have found some ways for themselves which work to eliminate past learned responses" (Sargent 15 1987). For those who want to find ways to unhook from their passed learned experiences, the D.C.P. offers Unlearning.

There are many other applications of the D.C.P. and these are discussed in the next chapter on Applications.

Chapter 8 - Applications

There are many applications of the Designed Change Process and this chapter describes these applications and where and how the D.C.P. is effective. The results, based upon a bimodal view are often surprisingly different from other views of psychology. (Sargent 1984)

Using the D.C.P., three specific effects of stress and feelings are clear:

1. The associations between feelings and specific behaviors form behavior patterns that can result in undesirable behaviors.

2. Stress affects behavior by affecting thinking.

3. Stress affects physical illness.

The Applications

1. Change – requires Intentional behavior that is flexible and the integration of the Automatic behavior to unlearn. This is the core of the D.C.P. As people accumulate experiences, they change. Sargent describes this change as "a mismatch between ... the individual's expectations for life and his achievements" (110 1984). This 'mismatch' is a source of stress that results in distress and can be very disruptive. To make matters worse, the individual is likely to hold on even more tightly to the expectations that have failed. (Sargent 1984). The D.C.P. allows the changes to be made "intentionally", thus averting the disruption of life.

Just as individuals change, so too do couples. They often find that the basis of their relationship no longer fits how they would like to live. What is required is the cultivation of Intentional behavior to provide flexibility in relating (Sargent 1984). Recall that when an individual becomes distressed, the Automatic behavior is triggered which can include a number of behavior patterns learned early in one's life. The way that all of us learned to relate to each other is from a parent/child model. In times of stress, people revert back to either child behavior or "parent" (authority) behavior. Both individuals and couples change as time passes. However, the behavior patterns do not, unless one intentional chooses to change them. Many of these patterns can be rather disruptive to both an individual and to a couple.

As has been previously discussed, the tendency is for an individual to hold on to his or her expectations and continue the behavior, which is rigid, repetitive and automatic if the individual is distressed. Oftentimes in a relationship, both people are running behavior patterns that tend to feed off of each other, exacerbating each other's stress level and only strengthening the undesirable behavior. Frequently communication between the two people breaks down only compounding the issue.

The D.C.P. offers people a way of changing their unwanted behaviors by integrating Intentional behavior with Automatic behavior, thus offering people a way to make effective change. Included in this process are the interruption of unwanted behavior and the creation of a new behavior. Good communication skills, a solid sense of self ("ME") and the ability to change feelings are also an essential part of this process.

"The nature of human thought processing contains both flexible and rigid elements. The skillful use of these forces is the nature of the application of the Designed Change Process."

(Sargent 111 1984)

130

2. Healing the Body – Many physical illnesses have a stress related component which contributes to the illness. The D.C.P. has developed detailed information about the effects of feelings and stressors on the tissues and organs of the human body. For example, it has been discovered by Sargent, (1974, 1984) that there is a relationship between fear and stomach problems, loneliness and sore throats, anger and chest problems. While stress isn't necessarily the sole reason for such physical ailments, it plays a contributing role. If nothing else, stress aggravates an individual and in turn causes that person to focus on distress which only intensifies itself. However, such illnesses as hypertension, heart attacks, and many other illnesses can be greatly affected by stress.

You may have experienced visiting your physician and being in a distressed state. When your blood pressure is taken, it is elevated. Many people have "white coat syndrome" and experience an elevation in their blood pressure whenever it is taken in a doctor's office, usually by a doctor, nurse or technician wearing white. Once I was so nervous at a hospital that an automatic blood pressure monitor couldn't get a reading because my blood pressure was so high. A nurse had to take it manually. The high reading was due to "white coat syndrome".

Many years ago, we (trainees and staff) had a lot of fun with some bio-feedback equipment. By focusing on specific feelings we here able to make the monitors on the instruments either rise or fall depending upon which feelings we focused upon. (This was part of a training program at Change Agents). Since that time, a significant amount of research has documented the relationship between illness and feelings and specifically about changing the effects of stress and the immune system. A quick search on the Web using Google resulted in over 50,500 listings!

Here is how the D.C.P. can help people with a suspected stress related illness improve their recovery:

1) Identify the feelings that seem to be related to the illness by using the scanning technique.

2) Interrupt those feelings using a variety of techniques.

3) Select feelings that will promote health (non-distressing feelings).

4) Maintain those selected feelings by focusing upon them.

Selected feelings of a non-distressing nature have their own effects upon various tissues and organs of the body (Sargent 1984). Patients learn information and techniques which will "make connections between psychosocial factors such as feelings and the etiology and course of their illnesses" (Sargent 114, 1984). With this information and skills, they can find feeling states that are not compatible with their illness and practice them. Recall that incompatibility can be used to counter not only behavior patterns but also a variety of emotional states such as depression, anxiety and fear. These three distressed feeling states frequently play a role in contributing to illnesses. Essentially what patients would be doing is maintaining an emotional state that is incompatible with the illness and feelings associated with the illness.

Associations are built into this process so each step of this process is not an isolated act. With the use of imagery and associations, these techniques are integrated into the healing process. The "physiological and biochemical state will be maintained without the need for the patient to think about it" (Sargent 111 1984). The result is the new feeling state becomes automatic, as a new behavior has been learned.

3. Training and Education - The D.C.P. offers three significant applications in education:

    1) to change the intensity in the classroom setting. Most classroom settings produce strong social conditioning, which often results in undesirable outcomes.

    2) to evaluate the positive and negative effects of the teacher-student roles (which is usually a parent/child relationship with a variety of distressed patterns)

    3) to clearly distinguish the difference between education and training and the usefulness of each (Sargent 1984)

Learning which takes place in a stress filled classroom produces powerful patterns of behavior that often thwart the desires of the teacher. These patterns include learned behaviors that may include reactive or conforming responses to the subject content, the teacher or the authority of the school. They can also be responses demanded by peers.

The Process is used to analyze the roles of the teacher and the student and two main styles of teaching – permissive and authoritarian. These two styles are actually the same in one significant way. They are both parental methods of control. "The control is from the role and through feelings stimulated in the student" (Sargent 115, 1984).

The permissive style allows for the student to "explore and grow" (Sargent 115). However, the "permissive" style is still authoritarian and attempts to control indirectly, via various persuasion and manipulation techniques. Use of such phrases includes "You wouldn't want to --" and "How do you think – feels?". (Sargent 115). According to Sargent, (115) use of such phrases portrays the manipulative use of feelings, especially guilt.

Many teachers who use the "permissive' style of teaching have difficulty realizing that such an approach is a parental method of controlling. Indeed, many will argue that the authoritarian approach is very controlling and parental (which it is) in that one is continuously telling students what to do. It is somewhat difficult for teachers to realize that "permissive" education is also parental, but uses indirect attempts at controlling student behavior through the use of manipulation via feelings. There are some teachers who take "permissive" education to extremes and permit students to do almost anything in the classroom, even if some behaviors are totally inappropriate. Such teachers then struggle to command attention and when they do get the students' attention, the teacher's wishes are ignored. Oftentimes at this point, the "permissive" teacher will switch to an authoritarian style that utilizes threats and intimidation.

The result of using either of these approaches frequently results in rebellious behavior, or frightened or guilty conformists. None of these behaviors foster a good atmosphere for learning as the distress level is high in both teacher and student.

An alternative to both of these parental styles of teaching is the Direct Teacher Style – where both students and teacher know the limits of what is acceptable. Teachers using this style do administer sanctions when necessary, but without threat. When both students and the teacher are clear what is acceptable behavior and what isn't, students refrain from testing the teacher, because they know what the result will be. This is something that most students will learn very quickly. Using this style teachers are direct about the power that they need to make the classroom conducive for learning. Yet, they are also aware that "individual freedom is necessary for education" (Sargent 116 1984))

Unfortunately, many teachers threaten students with consequences, but don't follow through with them. Sometimes such threats are impossible to enforce, while other times they are an idol threat with no intentions of ever enforcing them. Such intermittent reinforcement actually encourages students to misbehavior, because sometimes they can get away with whatever they did. Authoritarians also use threats and are more likely to follow up with punishment and some authority style teachers do succeed in having an orderly classroom, but it is dominated by fear. While an orderly classroom may have a quiet atmosphere, the underlying atmosphere is one of fear and intimidation – hardly conducive to learning.

The Direct Teacher Style requires that the teacher have a strong sense of self ("ME") and be able to manage feelings and provide a low level of stress in the classroom as opposed to a high level of stress. While the teacher may use a number of automatic behaviors he or she will use Intentional behavior when relating to students. Issues of control, often deeply seated in earlier learned behaviors, are eliminated with a combination of these skills. No threats are used. Students and the teacher understand the limits and consequences and there is consistency by the teacher is consistent.

Teaching and training are not the same. Training is conducted in such a manner that each person is expected to learn what other people in the training program learn. Education is designed to expand each person's thinking and to provide information that will be accessible in many different conditions. "Education enables the person to invent new responses for new situations, while training is meant to give easy access to exact behavioral responses" (Sargent 117 1984). Both methods of learning are provided within the D.C.P. and both are necessary for success. Both require Intentional and Automatic behavior and a key component of the D.C.P. is learning how to integrate the two behaviors as has been previously described.

4.   Marriage and Family – undergo very strong social conditioning that requires the use of the D.C.P. to interrupt and replace behavior patterns. By interrupting and replace various behavior patterns, couples can free themselves from the strong cultural influences of society. These patterns can and often do have significant influence over how people relate to each other.

Initially, two people, whether married or not, delight in exploring new discoveries about each other. (Sargent 1984). During this time, both people use Intentional behavior. However, as time passes, they develop a way of relating based upon role training and the couple's own agreements. Issues begin to arise around these agreements and roles begin to arise, too. Behavior patterns from the past are stimulated and pretty soon, each person is relating to the other through patterned behavior as opposed to Intentional behavior. The intensity of past issues submerges present relating (Sargent).

Gradually, a shift develops in the relationship and the couple begins to relate to each other more and more through old behavior patterns and less and less as person to person. Suddenly it becomes apparent to them that the delight they use to experience with each other is lacking. "Simply stated, a rerun of pasts issues replaces the present person to person relationship" (Sargent 119 1984). Their relationship becomes buried deeper and deeper under past

136

issues as they spend more and more time relating to each other this way.

These old patterns can be interrupted and the couple can find new ways of relating to each other using the D.C.P. One of the first ways that this can be done is by having the couple re-establish their present relating and then interrupt the old programming. The way that couples can establish present relating (as opposed to relating via patterns) is by having them "celebrate" themselves, each other and the relationship. This exercise in appreciation (celebration) was described previously as the "Homework". As this is repeated and rehearsed several times, it eventually become a familiar pattern in itself and reduces the intensity of past issues. Each person learns how to interrupt his or her own patterns. After this has been accomplish and trust has been restored to the couple's relationship, techniques are offered for the couple to interrupt the couple's pattern. It is likely that each person has probably attempted to interrupt the patterns of the other person. Such action is ineffective and not helpful. The couple must rejoin as a couple and agree to interrupt the couple's patterns only after each person has successfully interrupted their own patterns and trust has been restored in the relationship.

A simple summary of this process is: appreciate oneself, appreciate your partner, and appreciate the relationship. The next step after each person has does this first part is to begin to interrupt one's own behavior patterns. Finally the couple agrees to jointly interrupt their group patterns.

Recall that all of us grew up in parent-child relationships. This is how we've learned to relate to each other. This way of relating becomes more entrenched and the feelings associated with the behavior patterns become more intense. The D.C.P. offers methods for interrupting these patterns and can effectively reduce the intensities of parent-child relating. Intentional behavior vs. Automatic behavior is clearly demonstrated in inter-personal and personal relationships.

    5.   Sexuality – involves a mixture of pleasurable and stressful experiences (Sargent 1984). It often results in changing back and forth between Intentional behavior and past conditioning. For example, "… creative and open sexual experimentation and it's resulting growth and development alternatives with … guilt, anxiety and other early childhood and social responses.

Generally, pleasurable experiences promote Intentional behavior, while stressful ones promote old and fixed responses (patterns). There is often a "… mismatch between cultural demands and natural sexual responses … (Sargent 125). The flexibility that results from sexual expression may lead to violations of cultural demands. This results in stress and pleasure which produce changes between Automatic and Intentional behavior, or simply fixed and flexible behavior (Sargent 1984). Early childhood learning is stimulated by various segments of society: parents, family, peers, legal and moral influences. It is no wonder that sexual problems can be very complex with all these influences and one's own patterns of behavior, learned at an early age.

The D.C.P. can be applied to most of the elements within sexual experiences. The use of pleasure in particular, can be used to develop flexibility in order to promote change. Ironically, the very forces that can produce dysfunction can also be used to bring about "balance, change or adjustment which may be wanted" (Sargent 126).

    6.   Industry and Complex Technology – increases the effects of stress. In ordinary circumstances, persuasion and encouragement can be used to

increase human capabilities (Sargent 1984). However, increased complexity is another matter.

A peculiar situation can result when self assurance is added to uncertain situations of complex technologies (Sargent 1984). The result is "... personal certainty about a distinctly uncertain situation" (Sargent 126).

In complex management situations, this problem is intensified. Managers who conform are promoted. However, advancement to top management positions requires one to be versatile and be able to respond to a variety of various social styles. The learned ability to conform clashes with the need to be flexible, resulting in stress which triggers more rigidity.

The D.C.P. offers management training, where managers acquire a degree of self confidence that allows them to risk more unfamiliar styles. They learn about these styles from their own experiences and through observation. Role-plays are used to enable managers to be effective in various situations (Sargent 1984).

Executives need flexibility besides versatility. Flexibility is " ... the ability to invent new social styles as required" (Sargent 127). Extensive self assessment and self ability is required. "The familiarity which result makes it easier to risk the new responses required by executive positions" (Sargent 127).

In complex technologies, such chemical and nuclear plants, there are often long periods where everything runs smoothly. During such periods boredom can result. It is during such times that workers need to use "... fixed responses which exactly replicate training (Sargent 127). Yet, during such times, workers sometimes become creative and inventive and can place the system in danger. During an accident or crisis, workers need to be flexible in order to solve a problem or inventive with a new situation.

Ironically, during a crisis or accident, workers respond just the opposite way. Instead of being creative and inventive, they respond with Automatic behavior as a result of stress. In fact, the stress may cause them to revert to an earlier learned behavior, which may be even more inappropriate and even dangerous. Training provides the workers with self-confidence to risk unfamiliar behaviors, to use both Intentional and Automatic behavior and the ability to reduce stress.

Sometimes Automatic behavior is essential and other times Intentional behavior is needed. The D.C.P. provides workers with the flexibility to determine and use the most appropriate behavior and action. The ability to know when to automatically respond as one was trained to do, or stop for a moment and use a creative, inventive approach is critical in the event of an accident or crisis. The situation can be compounded by parent-child ways of relating which has been previous discussed. The D.C.P. can address this issue as well as the issue of stress, which triggers these automatic responses.

7. Counseling and Self Improvement are the areas where the Designed Change Process initially was applied. In this application, individuals are taught ways to strengthen their sense of self esteem ("ME"), reduce stress by managing feelings and interrupt unwanted behavior patterns. As has been explained, there are a variety of ways to change feelings and interrupt behavior and increase one's sense of self ("ME")

This application continues to be a popular and very useful one. The D.C.P. has a website which offers information and online workshops. For more information, please visit: www.designedchange.org

These are not all of the applications of the D.C.P. There are many more and some examples are provided in the

Appendix which contains a collect of flyers that were actually used to promote various workshops and classes.

Summary

The Designed Change Process had its origins in a recovery process of helping alcoholics. By integrating methods developed from Alcoholics Anonymous and reviewing several years of research, the D.C.P. offers "a new way to mange human behavior" (Sargent 128). It has a wide variety of applications. Sargent developed this Process over the years and it has proven to be effect to reduce stress, change feelings, enhance one's sense of self esteem and interrupt unwanted behavior patterns.

The Process presents three general challenges:

1. It requires users to be aware of two functions that appear to be contradictory – Intentional behavior and Automatic behavior

2. To adequately understand the bimodal model requires some experiential learning as well as intellectual learning.

3. The bimodal model requires a certain amount of self-determination for the client or worker and that may make the professional or manager feel distressed.

Central to the D.C.P. is a strong sense of self esteem ("ME"), knowledge of how to manage feelings and an understanding of how to interrupt unwanted behavior patterns. To use the D.C.P., requires one to not merely understand the material, but to actually apply the various techniques. Specifically, you need to be able to "Celebrate your ME", experience distressing feelings and reduce them and be willing to experience a behavior pattern that is triggered by distress, in order to interrupt that pattern.

What is amazing about the various skills and techniques is the fact that they are learned quite easily and much of the learning is experiential. However, on the intellectual level, the material can be a bit more challenging. Recall how easy it was to learn how to use the New and Good technique. However, to comprehend the theory behind it was a bit more challenging. It has been my experience that people are fascinated by these techniques and learn to do them quite easily.

The D.C.P. is applicable to both professionals and lay people. Counselors, therapists, managers, supervisors, medical personnel and those working in high technology industries and in other professions can benefit substantially from this knowledge and training. However, the D.C.P. is also quite helpful to any individuals seeking self-improvement or wishing to make a personal change in their lives. The Process can also be quite helpful to individuals and couples wishing to improve their inter-personal skills.

"The Designed Changed Process represents a revolution in the field of behavioral science" (Sargent 130). It is my intent to *carry the torch* and continue his teachings and the Designed Change Process. Long live the memory and teachings of Tom Sargent!

BOB SCHOENBERG

Bibliography

Greenberg, J.S. 1996. Stress Management. Brown & Benchmark Publishers. Guildford, CT.

Hubbard. L.R. 1986 Dianetics. New Edition.. Bridge Publications, Inc. Los Angeles, CA.

Jackins, H. 1970 Fundamentals of Co Counseling Manual. Rational Island Publishers. Seattle, WA.

Jackins, H. 1978. The Human Side of Human Beings. Rational Island Publishers. Seattle, WA.

Sargent, T.O. No date, Training Manual. Change Agents. (Self Published). Hartford, CT.

_____. 1978. Levels of Feelings. Change Agents Training Institute. Hartford, CT.

_____. 1984. Behavioral and Medical Effects of Stress. Designed Change Institute. Hartford, CT.

_____. 1987. Unlearning. Designed Change Institute Publications. Hartford, CT.

_____. 1988. Agreement Strategies. Designed Change Institute Publications. Hartford, CT.

Schoenberg. Bob. 2007. Critical Thinking in Business. 2007. Heuristic Books. Chesterfield, MO.

Selye. Hans. 1974. Life Without Distress. J.P. Lippincott Company. Philadelphia, PA.

Websites

Bowen, R. *Antidiuretic Hormone (Vasopressin)* Colorado State University.

http://www.vivo.colostate.edu/hbooks/pathphys/endocrine/hypopit/adh.html

Dialogue about CCI

http://co-cornucopia.org.uk/coco/articles/commun01.htm

and

http://co-cornucopia.org.uk/coco/articles/dialogue%20Dency%20-%20John%20Heron.html.

http://en.wikipedia.org/wiki/Re-evaluation_Counseling

CCI Co-Counseling Literature (Europe).

http://www.cocornucopia.org.uk/coco/literature.htm

Co-Counseling International – USA. http://cci-usa.org/index_2.htm

Rational Island Publishers. http://www.rationalisland.com/.

Re-Evaluation Counseling. The International Re-Evaluation Counseling Communities. http://www.rc.org/.

Re-Evaluation Counseling. From Wikipedia. http://en.wikipedia.org/wiki/Reevaluation_Counseling

Sickenga, N. Editor. CCI- World News Service - http://www.cciwns.com/

Sickenga, N. Editor. CCI World News Services. (CCI History) http://www.cciwns.com/cciwns.com/index.php/theory-and-culture/theory/history-of-cci

Appendix I

A list of some of the programs that were offered at Change Agents, reflecting various applications of the Designed Change Process:

- Change Agents Description
- Client Directed Recovery Program
- Change Agents Life Enrichment Groups
- Change Agents Celebrate ME - Cover Page)
- Relating Outside the Roles (ROR) Cover Page
- Relating Outside the Roles – Description
- New England Humanistic Education Center – Cover Page
- New England Humanistic Education Center – Program Descriptions
- New England Humanistic Education Center – Stress Management (Cover Page)
- New England Humanistic Education Center – Stress Management Programs
- Professional Peer Counseling – Description

Change Agents – Description

We are a Connecticut-based counseling collective and consultant group, offering individual counseling and group experience. We are committed to the development of personal strength and awareness. Our work involves four assumptions.

The primary focus involves the development of a solid sense of person. Working from such a position of strength offers a client clarity and the ability to create choices for her/himself. We know that distress drastically limits our perceptions of who we are and of reality. We know that from a position of strength we can deal more effectively with our problems.

We also assume that all behavior makes sense t o the individual. We do not implement definitions of normalcy or abnormally. We are responsible to understand how our client's reality makes sense and t o understand our client's personal definitions of words and behaviors.

With this understanding Change Agents counselors begin to move in a direction unique to peer counselors. At this point, the client's work is primarily learning. We offer information about concept s of human behavior and skills which may be used in life situations. This is unique in that it eliminates dependency on the counselor for continued personal growth.

Our counseling is client-directed. Paradoxically, we are active counselors. Clients work in the areas of their choice and with as much stress and distress as they choose. The counselor's job is to identify and share information about patterns of behavior and feelings. This information may be used by the client in ways which are appropriate to the context of their lives. Clients decide what work needs to be done, and counselors offer information about how it might be done. We do not give advice, nor pretend to have the answers.

What we do and how we do it is both hard work and delightfully fun. We concern ourselves with personal growth, cultural demands, and the interplay of both. Our process is one which enables us to be in concert with our environment and to maximize our creative selves.

CELEBRATE YOUR ME WITH US

Client Directory Recovery – DCI

3 Columbia Street, Hartford, Connecticut 06106 •

(203) 247•1912

Designed Change Institute Inc.

The Client Directed Recovery Program of Designed Change Institute, Inc. is a self directed recovery program for persons who are or have been seriously emotionally disabled, and for whom psychosis is an element in the behavior.

CDR is based upon the fact that many persons who experience psychosis can learn to use it for specific purposes in their interpersonal relations. Their ability to learn how they use their psychosis (and hence their recovery) depends upon two major factors in human behavior.

1. Behavior. Human behavior (including feelings) has interpersonal meaning. Behavior which is repeated is usually repeated for its covert interpersonal meaning rather than for its overt purpose.

2. Feelings. Emotional states in the human being are usually carefully cultivated. Feelings which precipitate psychosis become associated with psychosis. When psychosis is seen as useful to a client, the attention to psychosis brings present the feelings associated with psychosis. They are cultivated until psychosis is precipitated.

In the CDR approach, the client learns to make covert behavior aware. Central to this is awareness of the changes in feelings which a person is able to produce. The modification of feelings and the interpersonal meaning of behavior are skills which every human being already has.

148

Our culture requires that these skills remain covert, hidden from the client as well as from those around him.

With these skills clients can learn to change behavior long associated with specific meanings. The meaning of the behavior is a major cause of the behavior. When the meaning is made aware, when it ceases to be covert, it can be dealt with easily. Other behavior can be substituted for the undesirable behavior, or the need to make the interpersonal statement can be reduced. The process is simple repetition, until the intervening behavior happens automatically, and blocks the original behavior.

Similarly, emotional states can be cultivated for their interpersonal purpose. Feelings arise as a result of their association with whatever the person chooses to focus upon in the environment or from the memory. The availability of variety at any given moment is vast. Thus, the individual can at almost any moment focus upon aspects of present or past reality and produce ANY emotional state which may be desired.

Life Enrichment Groups- Change Agents

Change Agents Life Enrichment Groups capitalize on your personal strength and the skills you already have. Our use of Portable Images serves the dual purpose of collecting complex information about human behavior into simple images, and of making the information portable from one life situation to another. The result is rapidly increased ability in ALL interpersonal areas, permanently learned.

Participants find that these groups provide a gentle introduction to interpersonal relations. They are nonconfrontational, and are safe for voluntary sharing of personal experiences and situations.

Each session offers:

Lessons and exercises to develop skills   and information

An improved awareness of self and a sense of strengths and direction

A warm and supportive setting in which to explore change and growth

Space for dealing directly with your relationships with lovers, children, relatives, employers, employees, and friends

~~~

There are three eight-week units. Each relates to and reinforces, but is not dependent upon, the others. One may participate in any or all of the groups, with or without intervals between them, and in any order.

CELEBRATE MY ME

including strength orientation, self validation, being in charge, personal patterns, and human sexuality.

INTERPERSONAL RELATIONS

including listening skills and co counseling, interpersonal patterns, setting limits, conflict resolution, and role-relating.

FEELINGS

including what feelings are, how to celebrate them (even the "down" ones), and how to manage them.

Next Introductory Session:

(call for time and place)

CELEBRATE YOUR **ME**
WITH **US**

CHANGE AGENTS
3 COLUMBIA STREET
HARTFORD, CONN. 06106
PHONE (203) 247-1912

152

R O R

TRAINING
FOR
MEDICAL
PERSONNEL

Designed Change Institute Inc.

3 COLUMBIA STREET, HARTFORD, CONNECTICUT 06106

TELEPHONE (203) 247-1912

Relating Outside the Roles (ROR) - Program Description

The ROR Program

The Relating outside the Roles Program is an intensive training program designed for medical personnel. The training includes both information and experience which enable participants to relate more effectively to patients and to one another on a person to person basis, when that form of relating seems preferable to the more efficient role relationships. In an effort to reinstate some of the personal touch of the past, and to give increasing consideration to human aspects, the fast growing and changing field of medicine has made significant moves towards humanizing its methods. In spite of this, the accelerating rate of cultural and technological change has outdistanced these efforts.

The doctor in today's world is confronted with change which makes increasing demands upon professional time. Unreasonable amounts of new information about pharmacology, radiology, surgery, medical advances, and concern for more complete patient health records, interrupt the course of seeing the patient. Increased mobility, demanding more time for records, makes matters even worse. The ROR Program is designed to give the doctor an able assistant, when such an assistant would be useful -the patient, equipped with skills and knowledge about his ' condition.

Frequently patient skills are used to obstruct the healing process. ROR explores how and when the role relationship between doctor and patient works well, and it explores when a personal relationship would work better. It gives information and develops skills in quickly identifying when the doctor needs to take the lead, or when the patient may have important input. Many physicians have discovered that an aware patient can be a decisive factor in recovery, and that a dependent patient can be an additional obstacle to the healing process. It is also experienced that the dependency relationship can return even when both the doctor and the patient intend that it not exist. ROR equips the medical person to deal with this, and to cultivate whatever form of relating seems best at the moment. In addition, it trains the participant to teach the patient quickly and efficiently to take an appropriate part in the healing process.

The purpose of ROR is to give medical personnel increased choice and freedom in relationships with one another and with patients.

Workshops and consultations are available for medical schools, groups, associations and individuals. Bernadette K. Ryan, R.N., ROR Program Director Thomas O. Sargent, M.Ed., Consultant

3 Columbia Street, Hartford, Connecticut 06106

(203) 247-1912

New England Humanistic Education Center
(NEHEC) – cover

NEHEC

NEW ENGLAND
HUMANISTIC EDUCATION
CENTER

3 Columbia Street
Hartford, Conn. 06492
247-1912   106

New England Humanistic Education Center, (NEHEC), Description

VALUES CLARIFICATION

Values Clarification is a safe and simple introduction to humanistic education. It develops awareness and meaning for educational subject matter, in the participant's life. The workshop gives an opportunity to use the Values Strategies, as developed by Sid Simon et al, and to experience their effect. Our trainers are members of the Humanistic Education Network.

PEER COUNSELOR TRAINING

Our approach to counseling is client-directed, concentrating on strengths and action, rather than interpretive and analytical, advice-giving or confrontational. We teach our trainees skills and information they can use in their own lives. Once these skills are internalized, peer counselors can teach this process to others. We use the unique process of co-counseling as part of our training program. This enables our participants to share time equally as counselor and client. The training program can be tailored to meet the specific needs of your group or organization. All day seminars, workshops or on-going training sessions can be arranged.

PERSONAL AWARENESS

The information about human behavior that is presented enables people to deal more successfully with changes in their lives. Reducing distress, identifying and managing feelings, effective interaction, and intentional behavior are developed in a series of classes. The focus is on personal strength and an expansion of existing skills.

SEX EDUCATION

A major concern of this seminar is how distress about sexuality will distort the student's knowledge about sex. We will deal directly with that distress, as well as develop adequate sources for accurate information.

DRUG AND ALCOHOL EDUCATION

The purpose of this seminar is to shift the orientation about drugs from their chemistry to a focus on those social and personal forces which produce alcohol and drug abuse.

New England Humanistic Education Center, (NEHEC), Cover

NE**H**EC

NEW ENGLAND
HUMANISTIC EDUCATION
CENTER

STRESS

MANAGEMENT

PROGRAMS

3 COLUMBIA STREET

HARTFORD, CONNECTICUT 06106

(203) 247-1912

New England Humanistic Education Center, (NEHEC).

Descriptions

Stress management

(accredited)

This course explores and develops theoretical and practical applications of stress management. Participants will receive a variety of specific stress reduction techniques. Each class will be didactic and experiential in nature. The duration of the course is 27 hours and it carries three credits.

Stress management workshop

This workshop provides practical information what stress is, the effects of stress, and stress management techniques. It is a modified version of our accredited stress management course. The workshop is experiential in nature providing opportunities for actual skills development. Emphasis will be on techniques to reduce stress.

Each workshop is individually tailored to meet your organizational needs

Distress in learning

The focus of this workshop is on the effects of distress, how it interferes with learning, and what can be done about it. Participants will receive a variety of techniques for reducing stress. A portion of the workshop will be devoted to finding alternatives to those situations in the learning process that produced distress.

Test anxiety.

This workshop provides educators with simple techniques that can be employed in the classroom to help lower students' anxiety about taking tests. "Test anxiety" produces an inability to concentrate and think clearly. This often results in poor or failing grades the workshop enables educators to help students reduce their anxiety about taking tests. NEHEC is available to provide this training directly to students

Speaking on stress

A brief presentation about stress and stress reduction is available for your agency or organization.

Young People's workshop

A stress management workshops specifically designed for young people parenthesis ages 12 – 18 and parenthesis is now available for your school or youth group. Included in this workshop are ways to reduce pure pressure as well as other types of pressure students are facing each day. The workshop will also provide techniques for fostering positive self-image and self-esteem.

Professional Peer Counseling – Description

Designed Change Institute Inc.

3 COLUMBIA STREET, HARTFORD, CONNECTICUT 06106 TELEPHONE (203) 247-1912

Professional Peer Counseling (PPC) Program

Designed Change Institute, Inc. will develop a collaboration between several insurance companies and other interested parties to pool their knowledge and interest to produce a study of the effect of peer counseling in the field of emotional disability.

Phase 1. Preliminary feasibility study. Through a study of the literature, data already in the possession of the insurance companies, and through case studies of files of persons who are receiving insurance disability and treatment benefits, the question of the usefulness of minimally trained l ay counselors instead of highly trained professionals will be evaluated, especially in light of the cost of treatment related to the effectiveness.

Phase 2. Training and Direct Services. Peer counselors will be selected and trained. They will be enabled to give direct services to the emotionally disabled in a fashion similar to the ways that psychiatric services are now being given to clients of insurance companies.

Phase 3. Evaluation. This phase will consist of studies of the effects of such intervention through "peers". Several methods of evaluating the results should be used, as: Case study; an evaluation team, including mental health professionals and others; an actuarial study.

This study is being undertaken as a major public service. The results will be of great interest to the future of the helping professions, with implications in the benefits to consumers, the questions of proprietary aspects of

162

licensing and certifying counselors and professionals, and the more open development of therapeutic and counseling technique. Insurance companies, federal, state and local governments and consumers are being asked to pay increasingly large amounts for counseling and therapy services which may be of no value at all.

Increasing evidence mounts that • professional services in these areas are not successful in achieving their aims. Widely demonstrated alternatives are beginning to identify successful approaches in several areas. In the field of alcoholism the use of Alcoholics Anonymous, and later of minimally trained peer counselors, many recovered alcoholics, has proven effective. The savings to those who provide such health care could be staggering.

The program also will develop some guidelines regarding competency, supervision, accountability, certification and licensing, with a special focus on the benefits to the consumer. We expect these guidelines will of necessity be interesting alternatives to those technical and academic guidelines now universally applied to these areas. We believe also that this study will lay the field open to the innovation of new approaches to counseling and therapy which can happen no other way.

Thomas O. Sargent, Director 8-11-76

Appendix II

Biographical Sketch of Tom Sargent

Rev Thomas Owen Sargent (1998 photo)

[Reprinted by permission from Linda Sargent Reinfeld]

http://www.sargentrivia.com/My.Family/p1.htm

Tom Sargent ran a counseling and consulting center called Change Agents, located at 3 Columbia St, Hartford, CT. The building was part of a row house. The first floor consisted of an apartment that had been converted into office spaces and a room for conducting workshops and classes. There was also a kitchen and two smaller offices. Upstairs on the 2nd floor was Tom's office which was right over the large room and was the same size. The remainder of that floor consisted of an apartment with a bathroom next to Tom's office, with a sign on it clearly indicating that it was a private bathroom, part of the apartment. On the 3rd floor was another apartment. The basement of Change Agents was partially furnished but one had to walk by a scary looking furnace to get to the room. That room wasn't used that often.

In addition to providing one-on-one counseling sessions, Tom ran three groups that he called "Life Enrichment Groups" and later changed the name "group" to workshop. One was called "Celebrate ME", which was a self-esteem training and enhancement group. Another was called "Feelings" and taught people what feelings were and how to change them. The third group was called "Inter-Personal Relations" and dealt with that topic and behavior patterns. These three groups would become the three pillars of what would become known as the "Designed Change Process". In addition to these three groups there was a special group run for children. Tom once commented that the kids requested that the group meet on a Friday afternoon, so that they would have sometime to look forward to during the week. It was difficult for staff to meet at this time, but they did.

Throughout the years there were several different organizations and programs that Tom created. At one point there were well over a dozen different programs or organizations. Some of these organizations are represented in the Appendix and include the actual flyers that were created and used to market various programs. He originally conducted a training program known as the "Institute" This was conducted on Saturdays from 9 am – 5 pm two weeks in a row and then two weeks off. There was so much information that people received that Tom deliberately scheduled the training sessions that way. Eventually, this "Training" would become known as the "Change Agents Training Institute. Both the groups and the Training Institute were described earlier in this book.

Tom created the *Designed Change Process* which he described in technical detail in his self published book, The Behavioral and Medical Effects of Stress, (Sargent 1984).

After Tom "retired" from Change Agents and closed the Center he moved to Virginia City, Montana and become a real local folk hero. In fact, the Virginia City Preservation Alliance has a section of their website permanently dedicated to Tom Sargent, who served on the

Board of Directors, established the Virginia City Preservation Alliance web site and was responsible for initiating the Victorian Ball programs.

(http://www.virginiacity.com/#history).

Obituary of Tom Sargent

VIRGINIA CITY — Thomas O. Sargent, 80, of Virginia City, died Saturday, Oct. 20, 2007, as the result of a massive stroke.

Tom was born Jan. 3, 1927, at Hartford, Conn., to Thomas D. and Elizabeth (Owen) Sargent. He attended St. Paul's prep school in Concord, N.H., and served in the Navy from 1945 to 1946. He earned his bachelor's degree from Yale in 1951 and later received his master's of divinity degree from Yale. He was ordained an Episcopal priest in 1954. He later earned a master's degree in education from Hartford. He was truly a student of life throughout his life. Tom served in Anaconda as an Episcopal priest and was ordained as a Bishop of the Church of God in 1976. He was the Bishop of Magdalene Chapel in Connecticut and Montana. He joined the Industrial Workers of the World in 1984. Tom also founded the Designed Change Institute and Change Agents Counseling Center in Hartford.

He was preceded in death by his parents.

Survivors include his sons, Owen Sargent of Huntington, N.Y., and Peter T. Sargent of Gardner, Mass.; daughter and son-in-law, Mary S. and Doug Lloyd of Milford, Mass.; daughter and partner, Cathy Sargent and Laura Mele of North Hampton, Mass.; grandchildren, Peter Sargent Jr., Adelaide Sargent, Jason Lloyd, Christopher Lloyd, and Jasper Benjamin Sargent; brother, Joseph D. Sargent of West Hartford, Conn.; good friends, Bernadette Kelley, Lillian Evans of Missoula, and Bob

Drayer; and many special and beloved friends the world over.

Memorials: Virginia City Preservation Alliance.

[Reprinted by permission from *The Montana Standard, Butte, Mont.*].

Funeral services were held at St. Paul's Episcopal Church in Virginia City, with the Rev. Todd Young officiating. Interment with military honors followed at Hillside Cemetery in Virginia City.

About the Author:

Bob Schoenberg is a professor of Critical & Creative Thinking and teaches an online graduate course in Critical Thinking at the University of Massachusetts at Boston. He is also an expert and the leading authority on *Designed Change Process* and serves as a training specialist, conducting workshops on Critical Thinking and on *Designed Change*, both in person and online.

Mr. Schoenberg personally trained and studied with Tom Sargent, the man who created the Designed Change Process and has been a training specialist for over 30 years. He is also the author of <u>Critical Thinking in Business</u>.

Bob has an extensive background in training and curriculum development.. Combining his background in training, education, curriculum development, he provides a comprehensive and highly effective online experience for all his students. He created an online training program for faculty at the University of Massachusetts at Boston and is the author of the article *Student Collaboration Online in a Critical Thinking Course*. Participants of his classes and training programs frequently describe his teaching/ training as practical, effective and enjoyable.

You can reach Bob by email at: Bobsch3@gmail.com or Bob.Schoenberg@umb.edu.

Other Books by Bob Schoenberg

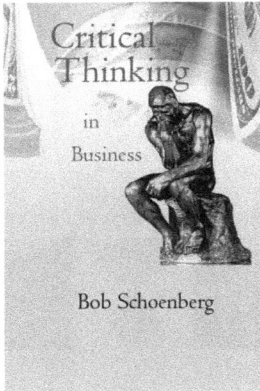

An MBA is not enough.

While there are a number of business schools that recognize the importance of critical thinking, few, if any, offer a specific course in critical thinking. Faculty members are experts in their respective fields: accounting, finance, management, marketing, sales, etc. But critical thinking, although interdisciplinary, is not specifically a business skill. Yet, successful business people do use critical thinking.

In this book, Bob Schoenberg, a recognized teacher and consultant on critical thinking skills, outlines key tools and attitudes to help think more effectively about common business issues.

From assumptions to frames of reference to ethics, critical thinking is the key to more effective business decisions.